BOAT BUILDER

BOAT BUILDER

The Story of Robert Fulton

By

Clara Ingram Judson

Illustrated by

Armstrong Sperry

New York
Charles Scribner's Sons
1949

Contents

BOAT BUILDER

ROBERT FULTON

1765 ⟷ 1815

Robert Starts to School

THE iron crane creaked as the porridge pot swung from the fire. Robert stirred uneasily and, waking, thought, "That crane needs greasing. I'll fix it this morning." Instantly, he was awake. *This* morning there would be no time for odd jobs. Greasing must wait until later. *This* morning he was to start to school!

He tossed off the warm homespun blanket, slid from his small bed, pulled on his clothes and hurried down the steep stairs. Early as it was, his mother was before him. Already the warm blaze in the fireplace had taken the chill from the room and dawn was making gray patches of the windows. Fragrant steam came from the porridge pot and dishes made a cheerful clatter as Mrs. Fulton set the porridge bowls from the cupboard.

"I'll draw the water," said Robert. He gave his mother a quick hug and then reached for the two buckets. "I'll learn about water, Mother, don't you think I shall? How it gets in the well ever puzzles me. And pulling it up with a rope—that's a slow way."

"None of your wondering this morning, son," laughed his mother. "Master Caleb Johnson will teach you what you need to know. I'm thinking that it may seem different to you, going to school instead of learning from me, spare minutes. So little I know! You must mind him and do as you're told, Robert. Fortunate we are that Lancaster has a good school even though it is Quaker. 'Twas backwoods and no school at all only ten years ago.

"Now I'll call the children. Mary! Isabelle! Come lay the table. Peggy! Abraham! Wash your own faces this morning. Mother's busy."

Soon the little family was sitting around the breakfast table; no one had needed a second call this morning. Robert was starting to school.

"You said we might have sugar, Mother," Abraham reminded.

"To celebrate. Yes, here's the bowl. Just *this* morning, son. If Robert is to get an education we must watch every penny. Two spoonfuls, there! That's plenty. Your turn, Peggy, then pass the bowl to Mary. There is enough for two spoonfuls each, I measured it. Mind the milk jug, Isabelle. It's very full. You pour Abraham's."

"Why mayn't Isabelle and I go to school, Mother?" asked eleven-year-old Mary. "We're older than Robert."

"Such a girl as you are!" Mrs. Fulton reached over and patted the strong brown hand. "Speaking such words when you might better be putting porridge and maple sugar into your mouth! You've helped plan, Mary. You know we must put the money all together to send my oldest son?"

Robert looked at his sister thoughtfully. "She speaks rightly, Mother. Her turn should be first. She reads and ciphers as well as I do now. So does Isabelle."

"A credit to me you are at that! It's a good thing my dear mother believed in some learning for girls and taught me herself."

"Well, I'm not going to school, Mother!" Abraham spoke up briskly. He had been eyeing the sugar bowl—was there a bit more in it? And could he spoon it out while the others were making this foolish talk? Peggy, a year older, saw his glance and gave the bowl a shove in his direction. "I'm not going to school a day. I'm going to be a fireman like my father."

Mrs. Fulton pushed the bowl in front of him, not a move had missed her maternal eye. "Maybe you can find a bit in there, little one. Take it openly; we're glad to have you scrape the bowl. Yes, I hope you will be like your good father, Abraham. But remember, he wasn't only a fireman. He was a deacon in the Presbyterian Church and a good tailor to support his family. You'll have to work to better his record."

"I'm a-going to, Ma'am," replied the little boy, awed by the sugar and reminded into his manners. "I'll help a lot while Robert's gone."

Breakfast over, Robert went to the washbench outside the kitchen door and scrubbed hands, ears and neck. Mary washed the cups and bowls at the table while nine-year-old Isabelle swept the hearth and kept an eye on Peggy and Abraham as they shelled the corn for the chickens. Mrs. Fulton hurried into her Sunday best dress. For years she had planned and longed for this day, planning education was not easy for a widow with five children and the tiniest of incomes, but somehow she had managed. She settled the full skirt around her still slender waist, pinned on her wedding brooch and straightened her lace collar.

"Ready, Robert? Did you wash back of your ears?"

Mary giggled. "And he so grown up he goes to school, Mother!"

"All the more reason to be clean," answered Mrs. Fulton as Robert came to her for inspection. Hands on his shoulders, she turned him this way and that. She looked at his butternut brown homespun jacket that she had woven, dyed and tailored herself; the fresh white collar she had ironed by candlelight the evening before. She looked at his curly, black hair wet and smooth with the brushing he had just given it, his arched brows, wide forehead and shining eyes.

"Would your father could see you this day, son. Right proud he'd be, you bearing his name and all.

Mind you be a credit to him! Keep the fire up, Mary, and watch the children. Come, Robert." She shut the door and they started briskly toward King Street.

Robert ran ahead a bit but as they came in sight of the schoolhouse, he walked close, taking her hand under her shawl as they drew near.

"Why is a schoolhouse made of brick, Mother? And do you think he will like me?"

"A schoolhouse is always made of brick, son. Would you have it of logs, so old-fashioned? And why does liking matter? School is not a sociable. You are to learn."

"I'll try, Mother. I want to learn. But liking hasn't seemed to spoil learning when you have taught me."

Mrs. Fulton smiled her quick Irish smile and held his hand tightly. "You are my good lad, Robert. I'll be missing you. But a man must teach you now."

Shyly she opened the schoolhouse door. Master Caleb Johnson sat at his desk across the room. As he looked up to see who was entering, his bushy eyebrows drew sharply together and his thin fingers tightened on the bunch of hickory switches he was holding. Mrs. Fulton walked to his desk, Robert following closely. He looked at the hand-hewn planking on the floor but, from the corner of his eyes, he noticed the boys on their bench, John Cope, Malcolm Ross, Henry Swift and others. On the other side the girls sat primly, Ellen and Patience Day, Abigail Swift, Sally McKay. How different they all looked here. There wasnt' a smile or a motion to show that they noticed him.

"This is my son," said Mrs. Fulton, shyly, proudly. The master frowned at the little boy.

"Name!"

"Robert Fulton, sir."

"Age?"

"Eight—come November fourteenth, sir."

"Thou canst read?"

"Yes, sir. I can write and cipher, too." He smiled up at his mother, gratefully. "I have read the Shorter Catechism, the Book of Hymns and I'm reading the Bible, sir."

The schoolmaster studied him. Was the boy forward? Or only intelligent? "Take this book and study. If thou art to speak, thou shalt be told."

Robert took the book eagerly, for at a glance he saw it was one he had not read. He sat himself down at the end of the bench. Mrs. Fulton with her quiet step left the room, closing the door behind her. The children breathed long sighs. Robert, their neighbor and playmate, was started in school.

The Schoolmaster Is Surprised

SPRING came early to Pennsylvania in the year 1774. Dogwood flung out its delicate green and snowy white. Pussy willows down by Conestoga Creek swelled to plumpness and then spring beauties, violets and cowslips made the woods and meadows gay.

At the woodpile, Robert stopped chopping to stack. A mild morning like this was welcome after the winter cold. A boy could work, now, without freezing his fingers. Since he had started to school, wood had to be chopped and carried into the house in the early morning for in the afternoon there was always some job to do, fixing this kettle, mending that lock, glazing a broken window.

"A good thing it is that you are handy, son," his mother often said. Indeed, only the night before she had exclaimed proudly when he succeeded in pounding a patch over the worn spot in the family porridge kettle. "Whatever we'd do without you, I couldn't be telling!"

Robert smiled at the recollection. Of course it was pleasant to be admired, but mending an old iron pot —what was that? Nothing, compared with what he meant to do someday. He eyed the wood thought-fully. There was almost enough for today. As he reached for the ax to chop more, his fingers strayed to his pocket and he touched his newest treasure. Just one look he'd have; that wouldn't take much time. He pulled from his pocket a rough, flat bit that looked like shale. He turned it tenderly, in a rolling motion and was about to put it back into his pocket when Mary called.

"Mother says that's enough, Bob! Come to break-fast. There's corn pone and fresh butter for a treat!" As she turned to go back into the house, she noticed that he had something in his hand.

"Have you something new, Bob?" she asked, and ran over to see.

"It doesn't look pretty now," he said to forestall her disappointment. "But you just wait until this evening! I'll show you something!"

"But what *is* it?"

"Black lead. I found it in limestone down by the river. I was certain there would be some there because——"

"What's it *good* for, Bob?" Mary was a practical little girl, never interested in causes.

"Nothing, now. But wait till evening. I'll bring you a surprise."

"Can you make it at school?" wondered Mary.

Robert grunted. "Can't do anything at school but

read the same books over and over. Never a question does Master Johnson answer. Maybe he doesn't know!" Robert chuckled good-humoredly.

"Robert Fulton! And him a schoolmaster! Of course he knows everything!"

"He shall know something new this day for I shall show him. But not unless I get my work done and breakfast eaten quickly. I must stop by the shop before school." He thrust the shale into his pocket, loaded his arms with wood and hurried to the house.

"You must go early, son?" Mrs. Fulton noticed the haste with which Robert was eating the breakfast she had planned as a treat.

"I thought to stop at the shop, Mother. But if you need anything I can wait."

"It's just the lye pail. I'm that fearful to let the others carry it for it's full to overflowing. This fine spring morning would be right for soap making if you could lay the fire and get out the kettle."

"We'd make soap this day!" exclaimed Isabelle, gaily. "Then we can wash my petticoats tomorrow. You'd not believe, Bob, how low this family is on soap."

"Mind you look in my pockets before you wash my shirt," teased Robert. "Remember that churn I carved so carefully and you broke in the washtub?"

"Oh, I was so sorry," cried Isabelle contritely. "It was such a cunning thing, too. Peggy! You must help me remember! Look in every pocket for Robert's treasures."

"No need to worry this day," Mrs. Fulton gathered up plates and cups. "We'll not even make soap if we don't get to work soon. Off with you!"

Robert hurried out and laid a fire under the iron tripod, back of the house. Then he lugged out the great soap kettle and with his mother's help hung it in place. On the other side of the house was an ash pit with the drip jar before it, at the bottom. All winter he had emptied ashes into this pit. Every day that the temperature rose above freezing he had poured a pailful of water over the ashes. Slowly, slowly, the water had drained through as lye and now the jar was full, ready for soapmaking.

"Keep away from this, Peggy! Abra'm!" Robert warned his small sister and brother. "Help Mother all you can, but don't touch the lye jar!" And with a quick look to make sure everything was ready for his mother's work, he dashed off toward King Street.

Mr. Isch's smithy was on the corner of King and Prince streets, next to Nicholas Miller's cabinet shop, right on the way to school. Robert often worked in the smithy, helping with the bellows, lending a hand and quite as often an idea, in the problems of making and mending. Now, even though Mr. Isch was too busy to be bothered with a question, Robert knew himself welcome. He went straight to the far corner where Mr. Isch had given him a small shelf for his belongings and, picking up a mallet, began work. He hammered the bit of shale and turned it; turned it and hammered. Anything but black lead might have cracked under the blows. Slowly, slowly the material took on a smooth, long, round shape.

The work went slower than Robert had expected, and of course he had missed his early start. But Robert was so interested he never once thought of time. He scarcely lifted his eyes from his work. The warm spring sun climbed high and still he hammered and shaped his material.

"There!" he exclaimed finally, "that's good! Now I ask Mr. Miller for a bit of wood. Master Johnson will be surprised, I'll be bound!"

It was a full hour later when he ran to school, still too engrossed in his masterpiece to notice the time of day. But as he opened the schoolhouse door and hurried up to his teacher he quickly realized that something was amiss.

"Robert Fulton!" Caleb Johnson was shouting. "Why dost thou come so tardily? Is it seemly that the son of a widowed mother should waste his time on the streets? Hast thou no wit that thou dalliest until noon? Lazy bones! Empty head!" His bushy brows drew together in a frown and his strong fingers clutched the bundle of hickory switches.

Robert walked straight to the desk, unafraid, and spoke pleasantly and firmly.

"I am sorry I was late, sir. I should have marked the time. But I have not been idle, sir. I have been making something of which I have need and have no money to buy. I have worked at the smithy, but I made this by myself, sir."

The old Quaker was taken unawares. His face relaxed into what was almost a smile as he looked at the thing Robert handed to him.

"You see, sir," the boy was explaining, "it's black lead, there is a thin strip down by the creek's edge, in the limestone. I hammered it out with a mallet and Mr. Miller let me bore an ash stick for the jacket. It makes a pretty good pencil, doesn't it, sir? Though I know I could do better again. This time I was too slow." Then, mindful of time, he added, "But I am sorry I was late, sir. I shall watch the hourglass next time."

Caleb Johnson turned the pencil this way and that. "It is a good pencil, Robert. Thou hast used good wit to make it. Often thy ideas are good," he added, candidly. Then he remembered his position and frowned quickly. "But remember! If thou wouldst come to any good in the world, do *this* day's task first. Then the new one. How wilt thou ever learn except thou studiest thy books? Now to thy work and make up the time thou hast lost or this shall warm thy back!" He flourished the switches and frowned at his roomful of pupils as Robert quietly took his place on the boys' bench.

Robert hardly heard his threat. The pencil was a good one, even the master thought it was. Just wait till he showed it to Mother and Mary, they would be proud as well as pleased.

"But I could make it better next time." He opened his book and found the lesson. "I must think of a way to make it smoother, and a quicker way, too. I wonder, could I melt it?" His mind turned the problem over while his eyes appeared to be on his book.

Major André's Paints

THE year 1775 was an exciting one for the colonists in America. The Stamp Act had been passed and visitors from the port cities of Boston and New York brought news of stirring events. Even in the backwoods of Pennsylvania feelings were strong on political matters. In the community around Lancaster, some twenty-eight miles northwest of Philadelphia, there were many Scotch-Irish settlers who were ready and willing to take sides against the British. The Quaker schoolmaster, Caleb Johnson, who was an ardent Whig, began to suspect that if he was to keep his living he would have to mind his words in such a Tory village.

Then in the autumn, General Montgomery captured Major John André while the Major was on his way to Quebec and he and his staff were taken back to Lancaster for safekeeping. The village buzzed with excitement. Never were chores done so quickly. Never was there such a rush to the Square after supper. Many an evening that began with news gathering ended in fierce debate as Whig and Tory argued for their opinions.

Soon Major André was allowed to sign a parole and was released from prison. He moved to the house of Caleb Cope, a neighbor of the Fultons, and gradually the children's horror of his red coat changed to toleration as they enjoyed his pleasant smile and thrilling tales. Then he volunteered to tutor John Cope.

"I must pass my time some way," he said to John's father, "and a lad of thirteen should be learning his Latin and French." Mr. Cope was glad to board the Major for such a good return and before long John began declining Latin verbs before the awed village children.

One morning when John went to his tutor's room for his lesson, he saw a freshly painted picture tilted in front of a row of books.

"Did *you* paint it, sir?" he asked as he looked at the charming scene.

"Yes, John. That's a scene near my home in England. I'm fair homesick for the place. See the church spire? And the lodge behind the trees? Though my picture does it no justice."

"You've painted it beautifully, sir! Do you see it in your mind and then set it down? May I watch you sometime, sir?"

Not answering at once, Major André looked at the boy's eager face.

"*You* want to paint?" he asked, much pleased.

"Oh, sir, if I could! Ever I see pictures in my mind but I have no wit to set them down."

"I shall teach you what little I know," promised the Major. "Latin comes this morning but this afternoon I shall get materials ready and you shall have your first painting lesson."

That was the beginning. John loved his lessons and showed an aptitude that delighted his teacher. The first picture John completed was shown to his friends and Benjamin Barton, a neighbor, was so frankly envious of John's opportunity that the Major agreed to let him take lessons with John.

Robert Fulton was away at the time the lessons began. Every spring and fall he visited his aunt at her farm and helped her with butchering or shearing or sap gathering according to the season. He was paid in produce and the food and wool he earned were a great help to his family. The day he came home the boys showed him their pictures and he displayed such intelligent interest as he commented on them that Major André suggested that he, too, join the class and hours were changed so Robert could come.

By this time war conditions made it very hard to get art supplies—oils, paints and dyes, palettes and brushes. On their fishing trips the boys collected large mussel shells and using these instead of paint pots or palettes they experimented with stains and dyes. Robert was a big help as well as a pupil now, for he had sound, original ideas and was willing to work endlessly till he accomplished what he set out to do. He had no money for brushes and after many experiments made himself a good one by painstakingly threading cat hairs into a goose quill.

"Now how did you happen to do that?" demanded John's father in amazement when he saw the homemade brush.

"I didn't happen to, sir," answered Robert respectfully. "I tried many ways of brush-making before I discovered how to make the hairs stay in place."

"But you've hit upon the right way to make a brush!" said Mr. Cope. "Benjamin West made his brushes something like yours. And he is a real painter since he moved to London. He paints for the King."

Robert's eyes shone. "That glad I am, sir, that I made them rightly! Mayhap someday I shall be a painter, too."

Unfortunately interest in his art lessons some-times interfered with school, for Robert liked Ma-jor André's teaching, as well as the subject, much better than Caleb Johnson's. Many a time when his face was turned towards his book, at school, his mind was far away working on a problem in drawing. Perspective fascinated him and often he squinted his eyes at the printed page imagining the letters now near, now far away. Often without knowing it, he moved his fingers along lines he saw in his mind.

One day Master Johnson happened to see him. He watched for a minute and made sure the boy was not studying his book. Then he roared out, "Come here, Robert Fulton! Thou wast never studying thy lesson! Come!"

The children shivered in sympathy but none dared look up. Robert, surprised and quickly obedient, laid aside his book and went to the front.

"Hold out thy hands!" cried the master angrily.

Calmly, almost as though he didn't care, Robert extended his hands and stood quietly while the mas-ter rapped them severely.

"*Now* wilt thou mind thy lesson?"

Robert looked squarely at his teacher's face. "Sir," he replied, quietly, "I come to school to have some-thing beaten into my brains, not my knuckles."

The words and the earnest, respectful manner in which they were spoken startled the Quaker. After all he was a good man and did the best he knew. He motioned Robert to his seat but when school was over he said to him, "Have thy mother come and see me this day. I need speech with her."

Mrs. Fulton delayed not a minute after she received the message. A shawl covered her working dress and she hurried to the schoolhouse where Caleb Johnson told her the story of Robert's continual inattention, his punishment and his startling words to the master.

"Then I sent for thee," continued the teacher. "He apologized manfully and said to me, 'My head is so full of original notions that there is no room to store the contents of so many dusty books.' That is a strange answer for a boy of ten."

Mrs. Fulton shook her head sadly. "I wonder if I do well by the boy. He is a good lad at home and ever helpful to me. If his father had lived——"

"He would have seen a fine lad," finished the teacher. "Robert is smart and will make his way in things other than books, I promise thee. Fret not that he is a dull scholar. He is doing well enough." Then his eyes twinkled in a friendliness she had never seen in him as he added, "But do not tell him his teacher spoke well! Thou knowest to be ever strict with a lad for his own good."

And Mrs. Fulton, feeling somehow comforted, hurried back to her home.

Whig and Tory

"Good morning, Mr. Isch!" Robert said as he entered the smithy one morning. "I see the new part of your shop is about ready to open. Doesn't it look smart? Now if you only had a good sign, sir."

"And why would I be wanting a sign, Bob?" Mr. Isch scratched his head, puzzled.

"To mark the shop, sir. A good sign would show as far down as Penn Street and every one would know this to be your shop."

"Hump! Don't they know that a'ready?"

"All Lancaster folk do, sir. And we're that proud. But so many newcomers are around. It would be good to tell them." He went on about his task.

Mr. Isch meditated. "What would you put on it?"

"On the sign, sir?" Robert rested the bellows and thought. "I'd make a picture of a rifle, sir—people are interested in rifles. I'd draw a handsome one—the sign should be about so big." He measured off some twenty-five or thirty inches. "It should hang from an iron bar. Your name on it of course, sir, and Mr. Messersmith's. It would look right handsome, hanging there."

"But it would cost money!" Mr. Isch suddenly

thought. "The wood and iron and paint. And it might be some work—" Knowing nothing of art he dismissed that part of the business as of little consequence.

"Two dollars, maybe. Three if you want a *very* handsome one, sir. I can just see it hanging there and every one thinking it was fine for the town to show off your new shop." He turned to the bellows and blew the fire to a white heat.

Nothing more was said about it all day. But as Robert was leaving for supper Mr. Isch motioned him to come near. "About the sign, Bob. While you're doing it, make it a three-dollar one. It's all foolishness—but think how surprised Nicholas Miller will be!" He slapped his knee and roared in anticipation of his neighbor's amazement.

The surprise and admiration, not only of his neighbor, but of the whole village, was well worth the cost. And Mr. Isch had the sign, too, a good bargain even for a Scotchman. The partners stopped their work many a time to admire it, that first day it was hung.

"Bob Fulton did it, you say?" asked Mr. Barton. He had walked up especially to see it closely. "Benjamin West couldn't have painted a prettier one and he's a *real* painter in London, now." The crowd nodded in agreement and Mr. Isch was still better pleased with his wisdom.

Others must have thought the sign a good idea for Robert soon had so many orders he had to beg permission to stay from school a bit to finish them on time. But the children had shoes they sadly needed and Mrs. Fulton proudly bought three pewter plates and a new loom. Robert must study nights and she sat by the fire, making scarfs and blankets by its glow. She always worked as late as he did.

The Declaration of Independence had now been signed and the colonies found themselves in actual war. The boys who had thought the arrival of Major André exciting now looked back on that event as a mild happening compared with all the stirring times since, for those years brought great changes to the little village of Lancaster. The firm of Isch and Messersmith got a government commission for making arms and doubled the number of workmen.

But food was high. Many, especially widows, had a difficult time getting along. Mrs. Fulton did not fare as badly as others because Robert was quick and bright and readily picked up work. He often seemed to know what people might want before they knew themselves.

As the war went on many British prisoners were sent to Lancaster. Officers boarded in the village and brought good business with their spending. But the poor privates, mostly Hessians, were a worry to the town. Many of the men were married and had wives

and children with them so the barracks on Duke Street, above Walnut, overflowed. The ragged men made huts to live in—huts of sod and dried mud and scrap wood—miserable-looking shacks that many a Lancaster citizen thought were a disgrace to the town. Men and women and children swarmed the streets, hungry and ragged, a real menace to health and peace. Housewives locked their doors in fear though they needn't have worried so much. The Hessians were not thieves, merely distressed, hungry, homeless humans.

Robert was fascinated by the mud huts and the strange faces and every minute he could spare from work and lessons he spent sketching. At first he tried to make accurate drawings. But the more he drew, the more the ridiculousness as well as the horror of the whole camp was apparent to him and his pictures began to be caricatures that were more startling than his earlier drawings.

Mr. Adams the apothecary nailed one up in his store one day and soon a crowd gathered around to criticize or admire.

"Where'd you see a fellow like that, Bob?" asked the clerk. "His bones are sticking through his skin!"

"Look at that coat, will you!" roared another. "A hundred patches if there is one. And each one different!"

"Look at that baby!" whispered Mrs. Cope who

had come in for a bottle of arnica. "His mother'll never raise him, I'm saying!" She stared at the drawing with a sympathy that reached out past political notions.

Robert stood at the side, listening, and when Mr. Adams spoke to him he said, "Look at them yourself next time you go by." And townsmen looked and were thoughtful.

Evenings in 1777 were lively times for Lancaster boys. After supper it was a favorite amusement to go down the street and watch the Hessians. Many a lad, either Whig or Tory, went home a back way hiding a bloody nose or a bruised cheek from a mother who had told him not to fight.

In an effort toward peace the village councilmen ordered a rope strung across Duke Street. This was supposed to separate the Hessian camp from the rest of the village. But instead it merely served to locate the scene of the fights as boys of both sides went straight to the rope and taunted each other into fist battles nightly.

One evening as he came home from delivering a sign at a small shop up King Street way, Robert stopped near a building to watch the crowd. Suddenly he unrolled a bit of paper, reached for his pocket-pencil and began to sketch so interestedly that he was late getting home. His mother was at the door watching for him.

"Did Christopher find you?"

"Christopher? No. What did he want?" Christopher Gumpf was four years older than Robert and an apprentice at the smithy. Robert supposed he had a message from Mr. Isch.

"Mr. Gumpf was going fishing if you would help pole the boat," said Mrs. Fulton. "I thought maybe you'd get us a string of fish. He said they were biting."

"I didn't see him." Robert hung up his cap. "I was taking Mr. Ross his sign, Mother. And then, coming home, there was a fight on Duke Street."

"You didn't fight, son?" She looked at him quickly.

"Not I! Never fear, Mother! What good does such a brawl do? No, I made a picture. Want to see it?" He unrolled the paper and handed it to her. She stepped to the window but the fading twilight was dim.

"May I see, Mother?" Mary looked up from her knitting.

"I'll light a candle. Hand me a taper, Isabelle." The girls peered over their mother's shoulder while Robert watched their faces.

"There's that crooked hut. I know the very spot, Robert. And that crazy hut with only three sides, next to it."

"Look at the boys, Mother! How foolish they

are!" Mary giggled. "Jumping over a rope to fight!"

"It's as good as seeing it, almost," said Isabelle. "But they do look silly, Mary."

"I don't see how you've done it, son," puzzled Mrs. Fulton as she turned the paper in the candle-light. "They look real, yet so silly, fighting."

"I drew their folly, not just the fight, Mother. Major André calls that kind of picture a caricature. I drew it because they *are* silly. What does a street fight prove? All their broken noses and torn coats are for nothing."

Mrs. Fulton studied the drawing again.

"Fish would have been fine, son," she said for she still regretted the missed opportunity. "But you made a good picture." She folded it over at the top and caught the fold under a cup on the shelf so it hung where all could see. "I'm going to take it to Master Johnson in the morning. He'll like it. He doesn't fight, either."

Robert flushed proudly. That meant that his mother thought well of his picture.

Rifles

CALEB JOHNSON was so pleased with the sketch Mrs. Fulton brought to him that he showed it to the village councilmen. Of course they knew that some street fighting was going on but it had come about so gradually that they hardly realized the seriousness of it until they saw it pictured in this vivid way. Immediately orders were posted in the Square. There was to be no more fighting and men with rifles stood by the rope to enforce the rule. In a day the village streets became safe.

Naturally this made the villagers talk about Robert Fulton, for word got around that his picture was the cause of the new peace. He got orders for two more signs, for the inn and the wagon shop. Then when he showed Mr. Isch a sketched design for a rifle handle the gunsmith gave it careful attention.

"That's a neat handle, Bob. I got an order only this morning for a good rifle. I think I'll use this design."

"Oh, thank you, sir," answered Robert. "And what would you think of making the hammer this shape?" He pulled a bit of paper and a pencil from his pocket and with quick strokes, showed Mr. Isch an unusual design for a hammer.

"Looks as though it would work," conceded the smith as he examined it closely. "Could you make it yourself?"

"Oh, yes, sir! May I begin now?"

"Bill Donnell wants to start east in the morning. Yes, get right at it." And Robert set to work.

At this time, the British soldiers and many of the American colonists were armed with smooth-bore muskets. But the American backwoodsman used a Swiss rifle, improved to his liking. This weapon was well adapted to sharpshooting where its relatively slow loading was not a great disadvantage. The frontiersmen had found that if a bullet was made slightly smaller than the bore and was inserted with a bit of greased cloth which they called the "patch" the rifle could be loaded quicker. When the rifle was fired this fabric was pressed into the grooves of the bore and prevented the escape of gas, thus increasing the force of the shot. They had discovered, too, that this manner of loading and the pattern of the bore gave the bullet an extra spin and hence a longer range. The colonial government had no money for guns, and each volunteer had to furnish his own. This was quite a contrast to the good equipment with which each British private started into action.

When Bill Donnell and three companions started east the next morning to join the army, Bill proudly carried his new rifle with its handsome handle and novel hammer, and young Bob was praised for the good job.

The firm of Isch and Messersmith had more orders, now, than they could well complete. Gunsmiths were not allowed to enlist for they were needed at their trade, and the shop worked every daylight hour, including Sunday. Only the patriotic zeal of the villagers made breaking of the Sabbath allowable in this churchgoing community, for Sunday work was practically unheard of up to that time.

Christopher Gumpf was promoted from apprentice to regular workman. No visitors were allowed in the shop (this was a major disappointment to Abraham and his friends) but young Robert was permitted to go in and out as he liked. No one gave a thought to the fact that he was not yet thirteen years old. He not only made designs for lock, stock, barrel and handle, separately, but for the whole rifle and soon he learned to design a bore and compute range. The workmen often called him "Quicksilver Bob" because he was so quick with figures, and asked him for help in computations. They admired the way he spent evenings studying books he borrowed from Mr. Isch but they, themselves, wouldn't have thought of doing such hard work.

Robert liked to test out his rifles before they had the official try-out. The Conawanga hills were over-

run with squirrels, both red and gray, and hunters were encouraged to rid the woods of these pests that ate nuts and robbed nests. So, many an afternoon Robert set a new rifle over his shoulder and went out by himself to test its range. And the Fulton family had squirrel pie for supper.

Mrs. Fulton learned to prepare the skins for use and made fine warm linings for the homespun jackets and coats the family wore that winter. But much as they profited by his hunting, Robert's mother worried lest something happen.

"I'm that careful, Mother," he assured her, "you've no need to worry."

"I know, son. But some other hunter might not see you. Every one's shooting squirrels these days. Mr. Matlack was saying there might be a bounty put on them. I'm fearing some one might hit you." Robert laughed at her fears but promised to be careful.

Mrs. Fulton was only half satisfied. She knew her son was not reckless but she continued to ponder the problem. Then one morning she had an idea. She hurried through her washing and got out her dye pots. There was some good wool yarn left—she mixed and boiled and spread the result out to dry, singing happily as she worked.

Two days later, when Robert came home from the shop his mother had a surprise for him. A new shirt was folded by his hunting knapsack.

"What's this, Mother?" he exclaimed.

"Your new hunting shirt, son," she told him, proudly. "And gay enough it is for any one with eyes to see you before he shoots!" Threads of brilliant scarlet crossed a check of butternut brown and white plaid till the fabric was so bright it could be seen at two hundred yards.

"Of course, if there were unfriendly Indians in the woods as there were when my family came out here, you could not wear such a shirt. You couldn't risk it. But now there are only hunters and I'll feel safe when you have this on."

Robert's eyes sparkled as he slipped the shirt over his head. "There never was a mother like you for ideas!" He paraded before her and then kissed her soundly. "I'm thanking you, Mother. And don't worry about me again!"

But at the regular shooting range on the common back of the potter's field the try-outs were more formal. On the day when a new type bore was to be tested, villagers and prospectvie purchasers as well as workmen came to watch the shooting. Malcolm Ross and Henry Swift were on the fringe of watchers the day when a rifle Robert had designed was to have its first official test. Mr. Isch himself fired the rifle, and when the mark was checked tossed his cap gleefully.

"That's the longest yet, Bob!" he cried proudly.

"Past two hundred yards! I'm that proud for you!"

Henry and Malcolm felt a thrill, too, but they were more puzzled than proud if the truth be told. How could it happen that a boy younger than they could do men's work? Not only do it, but accomplish it so well that men slapped him on the back and praised him?

But Robert soon made them comfortable. He came over and talked as quietly as though he thought nothing wonderful had happened.

"They're just glad that the design works."

"Then your drawing is something besides foolishness," remarked Malcolm. "My father said it was a wasteful use of time."

"Mayhap it is for some," Robert replied, tactfully, "though I doubt it. It is ever handy to picture the idea in my head so I can show it to Mr. Isch."

"But to make rifles, Bob—" Henry had wondered about this. "You didn't use to care about rifles. You used just to like tinkering and learning."

Robert nodded. "That was before the war. Rifles are needed now. When there is a need a person has to work to supply it. A person just has to, Henry."

That idea seemed so simple and understandable that Henry was satisfied. It didn't occur to him that soon he would see further results of Robert's study of arms and ammunition. Or that these results would seem even more wonderful than making rifles.

Lighting the Sky

JULY 4, 1778

LANCASTER was deep in the anxiety and distress of war on the first anniversary of the signing of the Declaration of Independence so there were no festivities. But as the second birthday of the colonies approached the citizens determined that July fourth, 1778, should have a proper celebration. C264765

There was to be no work, except of course necessary chores, and the whole day was to be festive in a way never before known in this new country. Families planned reunions; housewives studied recipes and devised tasty menus; new clothes were made ready. The crowning feature of the day was to be the illumination in the Square in the evening, and every scrap of wood that could be spared was piled upon a gathering heap.

The children were thrilled because there was to be a lighted procession afterwards. Every one saved candle ends. These fastened on sticks would be carried in the procession as torches. Boys practiced up on fifes and jew's-harps, and Old Man O'Leary promised to come down from his cabin on the Conawanga hills and play for the dancing that was to follow the procession. The village buzzed with excited planning in which every one took part.

Abraham Fulton, now a husky boy nearing nine, treasured the longest candle he could beg from his aunt when he went with Robert for the spring visit. Peggy, a year older, had hers and also a long straight stick on which to fasten it. Mary, now a tall, pretty girl of sixteen, and Isabelle, merry and plump and two years younger, would ordinarily have considered themselves above childish parades. But patriotism was different. They had been doing lessons and knitting by firelight for weeks so as to carry tall candles, befitting their years.

Then without a word of warning, a notice was posted on the morning of July first.

"The excessive heat of the weather, the present scarcity of candles and other considerations induce the committee to recommend to the inhabitants to forbear illuminating the city on Saturday evening next, July 4th.

                          "By order,
        (signed)   "Timothy Matlack, sec."

Returning from his work, Robert came upon a group of youngsters spelling out their disappointment. He read the notice through but instead of looking crestfallen, as the others did, he laughed gaily.

"So we're not to light the street! Well, I'll light the heavens!"

The children stared.

"That's impossible, Bob," said Mr. Donnell, who had stopped to read the notice.

"Nothing is impossible, sir," replied Robert, politely. Then he turned to the children. "Ellen, tell your brother Tom to come to our house right after supper if he can. Faith, I could use your brother George if he wants some fun. And Henry Swift— you may tell him, Sandy, and James and John Cope. But tell no others. I plan a surprise."

Excited though puzzled, the children scampered off on their errands. Robert laughed as he walked on. He must hurry with his dinner and get back to the shop. He knew the very page in his book that he must re-read to make sure of his plan.

Dinner was a treat that day; potatoes, newly dug and the first of the season, and beans so crisp and tender that they were delicious with Mrs. Fulton's freshly churned butter. Robert told the family about the notice but their disappointment was lessened because of his gay manner. Even yet he might bring about something good—one never knew.

He begged candle ends from the children, gathered up a supply he accumulated of his own and hurried to the shop of Mr. John Fisher, the brushmaker near the jail. Mr. Fisher also kept powder and shot.

"Will you give me some powder for these, Mr. Fisher?" asked Robert as he spilled his stock of candle ends on the counter.

"Will you part with candles?" the brushmaker was amazed. "And the illumination coming Saturday?" It was evident he hadn't yet heard of the notice.

Robert told the news and added, "Since the committee prohibit illuminating our streets and windows, I think we should respect their request. Anyway," he added casually, "*I* prefer to illuminate the heavens with rockets."

Mr. Fisher laughed heartily as he measured out powder.

"Such a boy as you are, Robert! Illuminate the heavens! As though the moon and stars were not enough! That's a good one!"

Robert didn't stop for more talk. He pocketed the powder and hurried down the street to the small variety store kept by Mr. Theophilus Cassart where he asked the price of the largest size of pasteboard. Emptying his pockets, he counted his coins and with the money bought several sheets.

"Good pasteboard this is, Robert," said Mr. Cassart as he started to roll the sheets.

"Yes, sir, your stock is ever good. But if you please, Mr. Cassart, don't roll the board. I shall carry it that way."

"What are you meaning to invent now?" laughed the storekeeper. "You've something new in your head, I'll be bound. Someday Lancaster'll be proud of you—mayhap!"

"This time I mean to shoot candles to the sky," Robert remarked as he walked out.

"Shoot candles to the sky! Listen to the boy!" Mr. Cassart watched Robert hurry up the street. "That's a fine yarn! The boy's good enough, but a dreamer."

George and Henry, James and John needed no second bidding; they arrived before Robert had finished his supper. But as he had brought home some work for Mr. Isch there was time only to set a meeting place.

"Can you come down by the creek the middle of the afternoon, Friday?" Of course they could, though waiting until then would not be easy. "You know the place," continued Robert, "by the big white oak." There hazelnut bushes and maples grew so thick that they made a secluded spot the boys often used for a rendezvous. They promised to be there.

Prompt as they were, Robert had arrived ahead and had his materials ready. There was a pile of pasteboard tubes, each about two feet long and thicker than a man's forefinger. Mary had helped roll these and they were neat and smooth. Then there was a can of gunpowder, a keg of clean sand and a small pile of tiny, paper-wrapped objects. The boys stared at the strange array.

"This is what we shall do," Robert began. He

picked up a cardboard tube. "You stuff in some loose paper so things will not fall out—so. Then you mix gunpowder and sand and pack it in with one of these." He took up one of the paper-wrapped objects and thrust it into the tube. "Put one in about every so often—see? Now you each take a tube and do as I do. We haven't much time and it is slow, careful work."

"But I don't understand," objected Henry. "What's the powder for? And why do you put in sand? And what are those queer paper things?"

"Blockhead! Dummy!" George snorted with wrath. "Who cares whether you understand? You're ever doubting! Robert knows what he's doing. Let's get to work."

"It's all right to ask questions, George," said Robert mildly. "I'll explain while we work." He handed a tube to each boy and set to the task. "Those queer things, as you call them, Henry, are fire balls. The gunpowder will explode them in the sky, and they'll come down as balls of fire. Of course the cardboard is just the case and the sand is packing. Here, George, you are ever careful. You may have three of these red balls to pack in yours. I've only a few red balls because the material is expensive."

Robert himself closed each rocket and fastened a fuse of string at the end.

The boys worked steadily and before suppertime

the rockets were made. Robert wrapped them in the piece of stout cloth his mother had loaned him and as the weather was fine, hid them under the bushes for safekeeping.

"I just wish one thing," said James Cope as the boys parted for home, "I wish General Washington was going to be in Lancaster tomorrow night. Wouldn't he be proud?"

"I wish the British were here," boasted John. "Wouldn't they *run!* I can just see them go!"

The daytime part of the celebration went as first planned. There were dinner parties and speeches on the Square and games and a shooting contest on the range. But the evening promised to be dull, for the councilmen reluctantly allowed only one small fire. The boys bided their time until dark, then armed with the rockets they had slipped away to get, they marched into the Square. Just as people were starting for home, Robert sent up the first rocket. The villagers blinked. Only a few had heard of sky rockets and probably no one had ever seen such a sight.

One after another the rockets whirled skyward so fast that the sky was brilliant and the villagers agape with amazement.

"What are they?" "Where'd they come from?" "Who's shooting them?" Questions flew fast.

"It's one of Bob Fulton's inventions, I'll be bound," said Jonathan Miller. "I saw him hurrying along this afternoon, grinning and busy as a squirrel in September."

"Did he think 'em up?" asked Mr. Adams.

"Well," Jonathan puzzled a bit, "likely he read about 'em in a book same as you and I have. But he's the only one that ever made 'em in these parts. Call it what you like, inventing or just making 'em, it turns out a pretty fine celebration."

Mr. Gumpf's Old Scow

FOR WEEKS after the Fourth, Robert was the town hero and even Christopher Gumpf with the dignity of eighteen years was glad to have him for a friend. Christopher was a regular workman now and Robert was promoted from doing odd jobs to regular hours and wage. Mr. Isch made quite a point of the step up and Robert modestly accepted the kind words and intent. But he laughed when he told his mother about it.

"Mr. Isch doesn't realize how much I've been doing, Mother. And now he will think I am earning a lot because he will pay it to me all at once. But don't count on much more money than we've had. There will be less time for signs and sketches. And the pay from Mr. Isch has been good enough."

"If there *is* any more," planned Mrs. Fulton, "it shall go straight into the ginger jar. We're saving money for your future, son."

"You've lots of faith in me, Mother. I'll try not to disappoint you."

"You've faith in yourself, lad, and that's even more important. And as for disappointing—there's a word we do not know.

43

"But we have to plan. You're growing so fast and earning well. It will break my heart to have you go—no, it won't do any such thing! What am I saying? Lancaster's a good town but Philadelphia is the place for a boy as bright as you."

"I think about it when I'm in my bed, nights," Robert spoke softly, almost in a whisper. "Benjamin West did so well there, they say. Do you think maybe I could, Mother?"

"Of course you can, son. And better. Don't you start doubting yourself. But the time isn't yet awhile and I'm not saying that I'm sorry to have you wait a bit. That ginger jar's got to be heavy before you start to Philadelphia, son."

So Robert worked his hardest. He spent long hours at the shop, and in the evenings he studied and painted. His only outings were fishing trips with Christopher and his father. A fine mess of fish made a delicious meal and was a welcome change from the plain, everyday diet of the Fulton family.

Deter Gumpf had an old, flat-bottomed scow and was an experienced fisherman. Indeed, he was *so* experienced that after Christopher went to work in the gun shop, Deter did little but fish. He liked going alone for his own company was agreeable, but the best fishing was up near Rock Ford, the county seat of General Hand, and the old scow was clumsy and heavy to pole. So he very often invited the boys to go with him. Robert enjoyed fishing and the eating of the catch. But the scow was so heavy and awkward to pole that the labor of such a trip was almost more than a boy could do after a full day's work at the smithy.

One afternoon in the late spring of 1779, Christopher and Robert left the shop promptly and with Deter set out for the trip. Each carried a parcel containing supper so that not a minute would be lost. The day had been hot and humid for so early in the season and it happened that Robert's task at the shop that day had been hard. The labor of poling the old scow up stream suddenly was too much.

"Seems as though there ought to be an easier way to move a boat than this!" He thrust the pole into the creek bottom and pushed with all his might. The scow moved but went straight into the bank. It was a trick, as well as hard work, to keep the craft from grounding at the many turns. "She getting stuck again, Chris!"

Christopher looked at his friend in surprise. It wasn't like Robert to fret and he always seemed to enjoy hard work.

"But you *have* to pole a boat, Bob. You couldn't sail a scow. You couldn't sail anything on this creek."

"Mr. Henry had a way that wasn't sailing." Robert had been thinking of it ever since they poled off. "He thought he could use a Watt engine to move a boat. Mr. Isch told me he tried it in this very creek. I guess it was a couple of years before I was born."

Deter snorted. "And what happened? The fool boat sank! I was on the bank that day and saw it go down. And a sweet time they had getting it up again! They had to work days repairing the boat after the damage that heavy engine did to it." Deter's plump sides shook with laughing. "Broke the boat in the middle, they did!"

"You *saw* it!" Robert stopped poling to listen.

" 'Twasn't much to see," retorted Deter. "William Henry was a good gunsmith till he ruined himself getting ideas." Mr. Gumpf puffed his pipe in silence a minute.

"Queer. Some folks thought he really had a good idea. Henry kept the model, you know. Hid it of course, folks made such fun of him. John Fitch had the same idea, you know, Bob. I saw him, too. Came here to see Henry's model and they fooled like boys over that toy. They'd much better have spent their time fishing. You can catch fish and eat 'em. But you'll never move a boat with steam. Someday they'll learn not to fool with such notions. Spoils a good boat."

Robert poled in silence for a stretch.

"Maybe it isn't the idea that's wrong," he observed, presently. "Maybe they didn't figure the best way to do it."

"Now don't you go getting silly ideas," commanded Deter. He spat into a swirling eddy. "Does a boy no good. I'll tell you, Bob, when we get near the pool up yonder, you and Chris have a swim afore you eat. Cool your head and it won't bother the fish so long as you stay down stream."

So the boys had their swim and were refreshed. But nothing could stop the ideas swarming through Robert's mind. The fish were biting well and he caught a big string. But his hands worked automatically. His eyes didn't see the pole, bait or fish; nor the bank gay with dogwood bloom and redbud and maple. He saw the designs he would draw when he got home—for he had an idea for propelling the scow.

It was dark when the three reached Lancaster. They locked the scow to a great willow with the heavy chain and padlock Mr. Gumpf used to keep his boat from borrowers.

"There now," said Deter, as the three, well laden with fine fish, stepped ashore. "See what we've got? Better'n fooling with ideas about a boat, Bob. Boys ought not mind a bit of work. Your mother'll be right glad to see your fine catch."

"You're right she will, sir," agreed Robert gratefully. "Thank you for taking me, Mr. Gumpf." The fisherman grunted a good night. It would not have occurred to him to thank Robert for poling.

He took that labor for granted just as Robert did.

Robert hurried home through the soft darkness, proud to show his mother his fish.

"I'll clean them right away, Mother," he said when she had admired them at the door. "You'll want to put them down in salt. There's more than we can eat at breakfast."

"I'm thinking you are tired, son," she remarked, kindly, as he set the light and whetted his knife. "Mary and I'll help you."

"You get the salt, Mother, and let Mary be. This won't take me ten minutes. I'm going to draw awhile, then. I'm not a bit tired." And he wasn't. The fatigue of the afternoon was gone. His fingers flew as he skilfully cleaned the fish, but his mind revolved around an idea that was shaping up beautifully.

"Going to do a new sign, Bob?" Mary looked up from her loom as her brother picked up the bread board a little later and fastened his paper in place.

"Not this time, Mary. I'm just setting down an idea I've got in my head. Likely Mr. Gumpf would think there was nothing to it. But he shall see!"

The Paddles Work

THE next week Robert went to his aunt's home in Little Britain Township. This was his usual spring visit and Mr. Isch let him off from the shop for he knew how important it was for the Fulton family to have the wool and maple sugar and meat which the boy would bring back. And orders were slacking up a bit now and they could manage without him.

Visiting his aunt meant doing a lot of hard work, of course, but it was fun for a change. His aunt loved him dearly and treated him as an honored guest. Often she gave him clothes and money for books, and always she listened eagerly to his talk. Days had been so full that Robert had not touched his drawing of a boat since he put it away at midnight that first evening. But he had remembered it and he took it with him when he left for Little Britain.

"What will you draw tonight, Robert?" his aunt asked as he opened his portfolio the first evening of his stay. "I'll pull up here so I can see you."

She loved watching him draw. It seemed like magic to see a plain piece of paper become a person or a scene or a pattern right before her eyes. Her

fingers were skilful at knitting and weaving, sewing
and spinning, but clumsy with a pencil. "Looks like
you're making wheels. No, they aren't wheels either."
She dropped her knitting and stared, fascinated.

"They are not wheels like on a cart, ma'am. This
is a windlass and these things that look like wheels
are really paddles." He put in more lines.

"See, ma'am? These are the paddles I'm putting
on now. They fasten on at the end. They will move
a boat."

"Move a boat! Those? Without poling?"

"Yes. You turn the windlass here"—he pointed
with his pencil. "The wheel moves here and the
paddles turn through the water and the boat moves."

"Now you're funning me, nephew!" She laughed
with easy good humor. "You can't move a boat
with a picture!"

"No, not with a picture. But with real paddles
made like the picture. As soon as I've finished the
drawing, I'll make a model and you shall see it."

She picked up her knitting. No use wasting time,
and she wanted to finish the jacket to send back to
Abraham. But she watched carefully as she knitted
and saw Robert finish the drawing. Then he gathered materials for the model, a board, some bits of
wood, wire and metal. And there, under her very
eyes, the model took shape, not in one evening, but
slowly, as Robert worked on it every spare minute.

The last day of his stay it was finished and Robert gleefully tried it in the great rain barrel. It worked! He turned the small windlass and slowly, smoothly, the paddles went round and round. The boat moved! It ran into the side of the rain barrel in no time at all! His aunt could hardly believe her eyes and she watched eagerly as he adjusted this and that to make it perfect.

"It's a pretty toy," she admitted, "and you're a smart lad to make it. But don't get to thinking that a toy is like a real boat that has to be poled. Shall you be taking this home to Abraham?"

"I'd like to take it home, but not for Abraham, ma'am." Robert lifted the model from the water and carefully wiped it dry. "This is a model of a boat, I'm saying. It's not a toy. I'll make Mr. Gumpf's scow work just like this does when I get home.

"But I could never carry this with all else I have to take with me. Anyway, I have this fixed in my mind. May I put it in the attic, ma'am? Have you room?"

"All the room you want, lad," she told him cordially. "And I'll take care that it's here for you next time you come. It *is* a pretty thing." She studied the little model, still puzzled by the way it worked, little guessing that before many years passed it would be brought down from the attic and set on the living-room mantel to be admired by visitors from near and far.

As soon as possible after his return Robert dashed off to tell Christopher about his model.

"I made it exactly like the drawing and it works, Chris! It works! We can go up or down the river with your father and it'll be no work at all."

"Don't you use a pole?" Christopher wondered.

"We'll not even take one along. Oh, maybe we'll need to push off from shore—you know we'll be going fast and the turns are sharp. But we'll not use a pole for pushing the boat. I promise you."

"Well, we shall see." Christopher's voice had no encouragement in it.

"That we shall," agreed Robert, cheerfully. "And we'll not tell a person, not one, till it's done and tried out." Christopher was willing enough to promise that because he didn't like the thought of the teasing he would get when the thing failed.

The two boys collected planks and boards. Robert begged and bought scrap iron from Mr. Isch and worked evenings at the forge until he had made a crank and windlass according to his design. They made matching paddles by fastening stout, slender planks at right angles and mounting a cross-piece at each end. The crank was attached to the scow crosswise near the stern.

"Think how speedy a light boat would be," Rob-

ert said as they fitted and hammered in the twilight.
Dark would soon overtake them and he wanted to
finish up that evening. "This old thing is clumsy as
an old cow. Let's make a new boat, Chris."

"If the paddles work, maybe we could."

"They'll work." Robert had no fears. "You tell
your father we'll go fishing about six, tomorrow.
We've only to set the paddle wheels and we can do
that in half an hour. I'll not bother about supper."
Robert was suddenly impatient as he neared the end
of ten evenings' work.

Next day Deter Gumpf was there at six, but the
scow was gone. A sound up toward the bend caught
his attention—what was that thing, coming toward
him? A scow that looked for all the world like his
but for queer contraptions on each side, was coming
toward him. Christopher was sitting at the stern.
Robert was standing turning something up and down,
round and round.

"They work!" Christopher shouted when he spied
his father. "The paddles work!"

Deter stared, speechless. Had those boys ruined
his scow?

Little Peggy Fulton and two friends happened to
be picking spring flowers in the woods. They heard
the shout and ran to see what was happening.

"Oh, it's your boat!" Peggy was thrilled but not
surprised at success. "Take us, will you, Bob?"

"Next time, Peggy. I promise you shall have a ride soon." Robert grinned at her happily. "Mr. Gumpf hasn't been yet, you know, and it's his boat."

James Wallace and Malcolm Ross were setting squirrel traps and they, too, heard Christopher's shout. They pushed aside the bushes just in time to see the scow glide slowly toward the bank as Robert stopped turning the paddles. Mr. Gumpf stepped aboard.

"You see, sir," they heard Robert explain, "you turn this crank, as I do, and that moves the paddles —so. And the paddles move the boat. It's very simple." Deter looked doubtful. "Want to try it, sir?"

"No, you do it." Deter preferred to sit. Even turning the windlass was labor. So Robert turned the crank and the scow moved along.

"Hi! Take us!" the boys shouted.

"Another time! Perhaps Mr. Gumpf will invite you," answered Robert. Then as an afterthought he added, "But if you ride, you have to take your turn at the windlass."

"We'd like that!" James agreed. "I'll turn it all the way if you'll take me."

Robert's success was greater than he expected. He not only was relieved of poling but of cranking, too. For village boys were glad enough to take their turn at cranking for the excitement of going along. The wonder of that scow lasted all the summer. She

was ceremoniously christened *George Washington* and Robert painted the distinguished name on the stern. Every pleasant evening, villagers strolled down to watch the sight as Deter and his guests set off up stream, delighted boys begging for the chance to crank.

But Christopher and Robert had to hunt a safe hiding place in the bushes to put the paddles each night. Many an ambitious boy wanted to try the thing by himself and the paddles might have been broken.

Robert enjoyed the success (and the easy fishing trips) but after that first evening his mind left the old scow far behind. If a hand-turned crank moved a boat, why wouldn't a steam engine do the task even better?

"I'm going to talk with the men who saw William Henry's boat," he resolved. "I'll find out why they failed. The idea's good. Maybe there's a book about engines." Night after night he turned the problem over in his mind.

But shop work, painting and drawing were bread and butter for the Fulton family. Robert never forgot his dream of a steam-propelled boat, but he did nothing about it for many a long year.

Off to Philadelphia

THE summer Robert was seventeen, Mr. Douglas, a visitor from Philadelphia, saw a portrait he had painted and begged him to come to the city and paint his wife and children.

"I'm going back next week," the visitor planned, "and I'll take you with me. I'll pay you ten dollars for each painting if you make them fine as that," he added. "And that's what Benjamin West got when he first started."

Robert had a long conference with his mother, Mary and Isabelle that evening. The little ginger jar had been filled and emptied into a safe place and filled again, several times. Mrs. Fulton drew the curtains and got out the money. There was more than they had realized.

"It's enough, son," she said, thoughtfully. "Maybe this is your chance."

Robert counted the money into three piles. Two he pushed together and shoved toward his mother. The third he put into a small canvas bag and rolled it tightly. His mind was made up.

"This will be plenty for me, Mother. Can you manage with that until I send you more? Tomorrow I shall talk to Mr. Isch."

That was a busy week. Mr. Isch was kind and agreed to let Robert go when work under way was completed. Three orders for paintings had to be done evenings for Robert wouldn't even think of leaving promises unkept. While he worked on, into the night, his mother and sisters were busy, too. Shirts must be washed and ironed, clothes mended and pressed, new socks finished off and a new winter suit made.

"You'd better get your new hat and shoes in the city, son," Mrs. Fulton planned as they worked around the table one evening. "You'll be meeting new people. You'll want to be stylish."

"Not much money will I have for stylishness, Mother. But you've an idea there. If I look like a city boy, maybe I'll get a better price for my work. I'll ask Mr. Douglas to send me to a good cobbler when I need shoes. But I'll bide my time on the hat. Better to wait and see what city folk wear."

"This shirt will need mending again soon," Mary spoke up. "Think you, Mother, Robert can find a woman to wash and mend for him?"

Robert laughed at his sister's concern, but he was pleased, too.

"Never you fear, Mary! Mr. Douglas has asked me to stop with him while the portraits are painted. That will give me time to hunt a good boarding place. Should I ask the woman, 'Please, mistress, can you mend as fine as my sister Mary?' ere I pay my first week's board money?"

"That would be good sense, so mind you don't forget, Robert," Mary replied spiritedly, pretending she didn't know he was joking.

Robert stopped his painting to watch her tiny even stitches. She was making his shirt band good as new. "I'm not expecting, Mary," he added, "to

find a mender as skillful as you are.'" Mary flushed happily as Robert turned to his work.

It was hard to leave but fortunately there was so much confusion that last morning there was no time for sadness.

Caleb Johnson came to wish his pupil good-by. Boys Robert had played with, and many grownups, too, stopped in to wish him well in the city. Robert answered the shouts and waved until the wagon turned at the bend, then he settled down to talk with Mr. Douglas. He would be lonesome many times but he would not miss his family as much as they would miss him. They would go on with the same old tasks and pleasures; he had a new world to face.

Before the Douglas family portraits were finished, Robert had found and moved into a plain, modest two-story brick house where he boarded most of the four years he lived in Philadelphia. Mrs. Douglas was delighted with the pictures and told her friends about the tall, handsome, young painter so Robert soon had more commissions. He painted portraits, miniatures and some landscapes. People wanted pictures of their homes and gardens; or sometimes they wanted a pretty scene to hang in a drawing room. Robert was busy. Many pictures of the country he knew best, the Conawanga hills or the quiet pools along Conestoga Creek were painted and hung in Philadelphia homes, and Robert grew the richer thereby.

Long before his first pocketful of money was gone he had earned more. He lived modestly and saved a part of every dollar. Whenever he had opportunity he sent money to his mother and when Mary Fulton married the nephew of the great Benjamin West, there was plenty of money for her wedding gift.

After a couple of years, Robert met Benjamin Franklin who was then an old man, nearing his eighties, but active and interested as always.

"You do well, lad," he said to Robert after he had talked with him awhile. "Your drawing is accurate and good. But if you intend to make a first-class artist of yourself, you should go to England for more study."

"To England, sir!" exclaimed Robert. That seemed moving along pretty fast. "I haven't been in Philadelphia very long!"

"The more credit to you for doing so well," approved Mr. Franklin.

"I'd like to go, sir," Robert admitted. "But not a soul do I know in the whole of England!"

"I'll fix that easily enough, lad," the old man promised as he laid his arm across the young painter's shoulder. "Let me know when you want to go and I'll give you letters. I have several friends who will be glad to help a young man. They'll give you commissions, too, never fear."

Robert thanked Mr. Franklin, though he thought to himself that it would be a long, long time before he could hope to go to England. But it came about sooner than he guessed. Four years of such continuous hard work as he had done since coming to the city had tired him. Then one day he was caught in a pouring rain and soaked through. Next thing he knew he was very ill and was ordered to take a long rest before he started work again.

"This is the very time to go to England," kind friends advised him. "The long sea voyage will be fine for your health, too."

That evening, Robert counted his savings. Besides supporting himself and sending money to his mother, he had saved six hundred dollars in the four years. He thought long and carefully and decided to go to England. But first he must travel to Lancaster, tell his mother his plans and let her have the celebration she wanted for his twenty-first birthday. As a surprise for her, he bought a fine farm near Lancaster and had the deed made out to her. The two hundred dollars left must take him to England and keep him until he began earning there.

The little house buzzed with happy excitement that fourteenth day of November, 1786. Mary and her husband and baby came to spend the day. Isabelle's fiancé drove to town for dinner and villagers dropped in for visits all through the day. Peggy laid the dinner table with the best linen cloth and decked it out with bowls of red berries and scarlet leaves she had painstakingly pressed with beeswax in a stylish, new fashion she had recently learned. Abraham did his share by providing wild turkey and plenty of squirrels for a pie. There were cornbreads and potatoes, apple butter and sweet pickled cucumbers and for dessert, fried cakes and apple turnovers with a tasty sauce.

At the end of the meal, as they sat munching Peggy's peppermint drops and maple sugar hearts, Robert rose and presented to his mother the deed to her farm. She was all but overcome with amazement and delight.

"You're ever my good lad," she said, happily. "Now you'll have no worry about me for on a farm I can provide for myself. And you'll feel free now for I'll be near Mary and Isabelle, too. Someday more than your family will be praising you, I'm thinking!"

When he left two or three days later, there were more visitors and good wishes. The village boy had gone to the city and had made good and Lancaster was proud. But no one suspected that it would be twenty years before he would come back to his own country. Nor that he would bring honor and distinction to himself and his country before they saw him again.

The Young Artist

To MANY, in those days, the long, tedious trip across the ocean to England was a hardship. But to Robert Fulton, it was a blessing. For during that journey of six weeks, he rested for the first time in his life. As he lay in his small bunk or tramped the deck on sunny days, he thought over all he knew of the great Benjamin West, now a famous London painter. And what he knew was both inspiring and comforting.

Mr. West was born in Chester County, Pennsylvania, and his family were close friends of the Fulton family. One evening Robert's mother had told him the story of Benjamin's genius.

"He was seven when he made his first picture." Robert recalled his mother's words vividly. "He drew a picture of his sister's baby in its cradle and the likeness was so good that any one could tell it was her child. That summer a party of friendly Indians visited the Wests and little Benjamin showed them some of the drawings he had made."

"Perhaps he drew pictures of the Indians?" Robert remembered he had asked his mother.

"Likely," she had replied thoughtfully. "I know your father said the Indians were interested in the boy and shared with him colors they used for painting their faces and their arrows. And they showed him how to mix dyes and get colors from berry juices and herbs."

"Then he must have painted Indians," Robert had decided, "because he would need bright colors for that and the Indians would like to help him. What else did he do, Mother?"

"When Benjamin was twelve his father brought him to Lancaster and it was then that he painted the Ross portraits you've seen, Robert. And not long after he painted your father's portrait and mine. Your grandfather was proud of those pictures, lad."

Robert had looked with new interest at the pictures hanging on the wall. He'd often studied his father's portrait for it was the only thing that made his father real. Robert was so young when his father died that he had no memory of him. So that painting was done by a mere youth; by a boy born in the country as Robert himself was born.

"And he is a great painter now!" Ambition had surged in Robert's mind, but his words were quiet as usual. "I wonder if I could be a painter, Mother?"

"Maybe. But he had many advantages, lad," his mother had said. "He went to Philadelphia and then to London, that makes a difference. Now the candle's about done. It's time for us to rest." She had laid aside her work as he snuffed the guttering candle. Robert remembered every word, now, as he lay thinking in his bunk.

"Mother didn't know, then, how many advantages I would have," his thoughts ran on, "friends, work in Philadelphia, the help of Mr. Franklin."

It was while working in Philadelphia that Robert had learned more about Mr. West, for the painter's friends there were proud of his brilliant success and liked to tell of it. He had studied in Italy for three years and then returned to London where he painted historical scenes and great, beautiful portraits much in favor at the time. He won royal favor and was elected a member of the Royal Academy and later president of it, the greatest honor a painter could win. He was old enough to be Robert's father and had begun to win recognition before Robert was born.

"I wonder if he will care to see me at all!" Robert thought, dismayed at his own audacity in planning to visit so famous a man. Then he touched Benjamin Franklin's letter carefully wrapped in oilskin in his inner pocket and was comforted. Work in Philadelphia had taught him much. He had already learned that a great man is more apt to give help than a lesser one and Mr. Franklin had assured him that Mr. West would like to help a young American just come to London.

But when Robert stood before the door of Benjamin West's home in London, he needed all his courage to make himself pull the bellrope. The house was a palace! Bigger, finer, grander than any Robert had ever entered in Philadelphia! It had not occurred to him that a Chester County boy could live in a place like this!

The door open, he was ushered into a large hall and Mrs. West hurried to greet him with motherly kindness. Soon he was talking to the great painter

himself and to his amazement was answering questions about Pennsylvania neighbors and feeling at home. Friends had written of his coming and both Mr. and Mrs. West were ready with a welcome and with plans for the young man.

"You are to live with us," Mrs. West told him. "No, not a word!" she added when Robert started to object. "It is arranged. We have ample room and we want you. So stay until you are acquainted."

"Today you shall settle yourself," Mr. West said, "and we shall see to your supplies. Tomorrow you will set up your easel in my study and start your work. Come, we will go there now and you will show me something you have done." Robert followed the artist through the long gallery to the great studio. Enormous canvases stood about covered with beginning and partly finished work, larger paintings than he had ever seen. Spaces on the walls were covered with sketches for the famous historical scenes which Mr. West was making popular. Robert was thankful for his training in Philadelphia; without it he would not have been comfortable in such a great house. With it, he could forget himself and show the master sketches he had brought in his portfolio.

Next morning they started work together and never had Robert known a man who enjoyed his task so much. Benjamin West bubbled over with enthusiasm and went at his task as though it was the most fun in the world. Robert worked hard and fast, not only in the studio under the eye of his teacher, but visiting galleries and seeing many masterpieces. In a letter to his mother he wrote, "There is more to learn about painting than I had thought."

For a few weeks he accepted Mrs. West's generous hospitality, then he moved to a room near by. Later he made several moves "for my convenience," he wrote his mother, but the real reason was economy; he wanted his money to last as long as possible so he could study. When it was gone and he must earn there would be less time for learning. Nothing was mentioned about the date of his return home but friends wrote comforting letters to Mrs. Fulton telling of her son's incredible improvement in painting and his behavior that was winning him many friends.

Robert tried to write to her as often as he could but as his funds dwindled even money for postage must be doled out slowly. Letters were costly. Sometimes those from America were put off at the first port and arrived in London with postage due, an expense far beyond his means. He was always eager for news but he advised his mother to buy the thinnest paper so the cost would be less.

In 1791, two of his paintings were exhibited in the Royal Academy. These were portraits of young gentlemen. Four larger paintings, one a Bible story picture of Elisha raising the widow's son, and another, a scene from Spencer's *Faerie Queen*, were hung in the Exhibition of the Royal Society of British Artists.

Benjamin West was thrilled about his pupil's success.

"You're on your way, now, son!" he cried. "You've turned the corner!"

"But I get no money for these honors," said Robert. He was proud of the feeling of success this honor brought to him. But honor earned him no bread and butter. Unless he earned something soon, he would have to take to sign painting or odd jobs as he had done in Philadelphia.

"Don't worry about the money, Bob!" Mr. West laughed happily. "Wait a week and you shall see! You'll have orders that will pay well."

"You're not to worry a minute this day," added kind Mrs. West. "I've invited a party and we are celebrating with you!" So Robert made himself tidy and enjoyed the party.

Mr. West was right. In a few days, Robert received an invitation to visit the castle of Lord Courtaney, Earl of Devonshire, and paint his portrait; and the fee promised seemed like a small fortune. So Robert packed his canvasses, paints and brushes and went by stagecoach the two hundred miles to Devonshire. It was a beautiful ride, that June of 1791, and the country bloomed gaily. Robert saw the blossoms, heard the bees and birds, and smelled the flowers. Somehow it reminded him of the hills around Lancaster; he wished the coach were taking him there. Wouldn't it be fun to tell his mother and Mary that he was going to a castle to paint a picture of an earl? They'd hardly believe!

The castle was even bigger and grander than he had pictured it. He painted the portrait in the great art gallery and the earl talked in a friendly way during the sittings. Titled men came to visit and the earl introduced Robert Fulton as his friend. They liked the young American painter and lingered in the gallery to watch him work. Fortunately that never bothered Robert. He enjoyed their friendly ways and gave no thought to their riches or his own poverty.

When the picture was finished and the money paid, Robert sent a generous gift to his mother. One of his worries while he was so poor was that he could not send money to her. Now she could rejoice with him that he had begun to earn. It looked as though days of pinching every penny were over and he was going to be a successful artist. There would be plenty for her and gifts for his sisters, too. He little guessed as he planned, that soon he would have even more success, but in quite a different way.

The Turn to Invention

THE change in Robert Fulton's thinking and in his interests began so gradually that he hardly knew when it came about. Talk of the titled men in the art gallery in the Devonshire castle was more exciting than any he had ever heard and he was thankful that he could both paint and listen.

Then, when Lord Courtaney's portrait was finished, the Duke of Bridgewater invited him to visit his estate and paint his portrait. The duke owned a great deal of land and many coal mines and was ever debating his two problems, getting coal to market and keeping water out of his mines. He talked about steam pumps and water and land transportation and many other subjects Robert had never heard so freely discussed. One of the duke's best friends was the Earl of Stanhope who was a scientist and interested in mechanics and invention. He ordered his portrait painted, too, and the duke suggested that the earl stay and have it done there.

As he painted these portraits and listened to the conversation, Robert Fulton began to realize that he was getting something even more valuable than orders for portraits, important as those were to him! These men talked readily of a thousand subjects that had hardly been mentioned among his artist friends in Philadelphia or London. Important subjects, too. James Watt's steam pump—the duke had actually bought one and it was even now pumping water out of his mines! Canals—the duke had had a short canal dug on one of his estates and was using it daily in transporting coal. He was pleased with Robert's interest in these new things.

"Water hauling is cheaper and quicker than pack horse," he told Robert one day. "It's a pity we can't have canals all over England. But that's impossible."

"Why impossible, sir?" Robert paused, brush in air, wondering.

"Because land in England is on so many different levels. You may dig canals all you like, but you can never persuade water to run up hill. But I'll show you what we've done."

That afternoon was the first of many visits. The duke showed Robert his canal, his marble and stone quarries and his mines. Robert, used to the free life in an American village, was shocked to see the hard human labor needed for all this work. There ought to be some way to save that labor. A few evenings later he modestly showed the duke a design for a marble-cutting machine. The Earl of Stanhope examined the sketch.

"It's a good idea!" he said. "Cheap and practical, too. Let's try it out!"

A small mill was built on the duke's land and was so successful that it earned Robert Fulton money and brought him honors from the Society of Arts, Commerce and Manufacture in London. Soon Robert had an idea of spinning flax and making rope, and both proved to be successful.

He was fascinated by the difficulty of getting canal boats from one level to another, and many an evening he made sketches which his friends thought showed good ideas. The visit to Devonshire which was to have been for the summer lasted two years and before he left his inventions were proving even more successful than his painting.

The Duke of Bridgewater obtained some orders for portraits for him in Birmingham, a large manufacturing center in central England. While there, Robert Fulton took time to study James Watt's engines, to observe new canals then being dug and to study many new types of machinery in operation in the great city.

James Watt's work interested him doubly because James was born a poor country boy, too. He was a Scot and in his youth so ill and frail that he could not run and play like other lads. Because of this, he learned to be skilful with his hands and to observe small things his more fortunate friends overlooked.

For hours he watched the steam in his mother's tea kettle and wondered about the power that lifted the lid or pushed a small article held over the spout. He liked mathematics and soon excelled his teacher but he had no interest in other studies.

One day his father gave him a fine set of tools. James loved them and learned to use them with skill and dexterity. This proved a fortunate bit of luck for when James was sixteen his father lost his business and James had to get work. He went to Glasgow and was apprenticed to an "optician" whose business was to repair musical instruments, spectacles and other fine articles.

A friend got James permission to read at the library of the University of Glasgow and there he studied mathematics and mechanics after long hours of work at his bench. One day a professor showed him a nautical instrument that had been broken. James repaired it so quickly and perfectly that he earned a new job, repairman for the university. Never had the fine instruments been kept in such good condition! Now James had a room at the university and a chance to meet and listen to educated men. They were all discussing steam. One even thought it might be made to move carriages, an idea that inspired James to more study.

The university bought a Newcomen engine (used to pump water from mines) for the use of the science classes. It was while making a repair on this engine that James got the idea of using the wasted steam to increase the power without increasing the cost of operation.

Watt soon made a model of his own. This engine was perpendicular and proved successful. But the building of the engine was a big problem for workmen didn't understand their task. James, though very skilful with tiny instruments, had never worked at any large machine. Then, once the engine was proved workable, James had trouble getting capital, for men of money had little faith. After many disappointments Matthew Boulton went in with him and the new Watt engine began to be manufactured. James then perfected a rotary engine and invented a steam indicator by which engineers could figure the amount of steam pressure. It was the work of this frail Scotch boy that made steam navigation possible.

Of course Robert Fulton, studying the Watt engine in Birmingham, didn't suspect that! But he was so inspired by the thoughts of invention that filled his mind, that he decided to give up his loved painting and use all his time for the new work. That was a tremendous decision and though it seemed to come suddenly, he really had been pondering on the idea since the first summer in Devonshire.

He went straight to London to talk with Benjamin West. Robert wanted his good friend to understand and to approve. When he considered all the reasons, Mr. West did regretfully approve but it is likely he thought Robert would soon go back to painting for he was ambitious for his gifted pupil.

Robert Fulton's whole life was altered, now. He travelled widely in England and in France. He studied Italian, French and German languages so he could read first hand the work men in those countries were doing. He perfected his knowledge of higher mathematics and science. And he made many new friends. He had a real gift for friendship, perhaps because he was always kind and fair and eager to listen.

Ideas for inventions came rapidly into his mind and he was able to interest other men in perfecting them, a point where many another gifted inventor has failed. Probably Robert's skill as an artist helped, for he could make simple, clear drawings which made his ideas easy to understand. In less than four years he had invented a dredging machine for digging canals, a system of inclined planes for lifting a boat from a canal of one level to another, an iron aqueduct for carrying a canal across a river and many other devices for quicker transportation of goods and for saving human labor.

Many scientists published books about their work and his friends urged Robert Fulton to write about what he was doing. So in 1795 he published two books, which were called treatises, about his canal inventions. His years of writing long letters had taught him how to express himself and his skilful drawing of locks, planes, and aqueducts, which illustrated his text, were vivid and plain to all.

He sent a copy to President George Washington and to the governor of Pennsylvania and to Napoleon Bonaparte in France. Six months later he wrote again to President Washington and in this letter mentioned that some day there might be a canal from Philadelphia to Lake Erie. Years later when the Erie Canal was built, no one remembered that it was first suggested by Robert Fulton.

But all the while he was working successfully on canal improvement and labor-saving devices, other plans were developing in his mind. The idea of making the sea safe and free to all nations fascinated him. Quick, safe transportation; the oceans free for all—that would make human happiness. He turned the problems over in his mind, dreaming that one day in the future he would do work vastly more important than his canals.

Fulton's Submarine

ROBERT FULTON sat at his desk in his comfortable lodgings in London. Tomorrow he would go to France. Piled high before him were letters and sketches and legal papers which his strong skilful fingers were rapidly sorting. Many papers showed the date of the current year, 1797; others were older, for he was an orderly person and kept important letters and notes about his replies. Quickly he glanced at each paper and laid it on its proper pile.

Those in one pile were about his labor-saving inventions, the marble-cutting machine, the rope maker and such; a successful lot of work they represented, too. The next pile concerned canals, locks, bridges, a dredging machine, aqueducts. These he intended to take to France, for his appointment with French officials next week concerned canals. Another lot was about steamboats; nothing had come of all that work yet. A copy of the letter he had written to Boulton and Watt, November 4, 1794, asking the cost of a three or four horsepower engine for propelling a boat, lay before him. He had spent hours figuring over problems their answer presented about size, fuel needed and other points. He would take those papers with him. After canal projects were under way in France there might be opportunity to work on the steamboat idea. He tied the package snugly with dark-blue linen tape.

The next pile was the smallest of all, letters from his family in the United States. How often he wished he might hear more from his mother and sisters and brother and the new little nephews and nieces! The cost of stamps was no longer a problem; Robert earned plenty of money now and sent his mother frequent presents for modest luxuries. But many letters written to him were delayed or lost entirely. England and France were at peace just now but only after weary years of war. Mail often had to be carried stormy miles out of the way to avoid warships. Even worse than warships were the pirates who roamed the seas, plundering and burning ships. Sometimes Robert went weeks without a single letter!

"The sea is no place for war and robbery!" Robert exclaimed aloud as his fingers touched the letters and he remembered the long gaps between. "The sea should be safe! How else are people to be happy? How else is the world to develop and share its resources?"

He tied up the treasured packet, laid it aside and reached for the last pile of papers.

"This will do it!" he said to himself. "When I get a weapon frightening enough, when I invent a boat terrible enough, it will keep both war and pirates from the sea. That will be a service worth doing!" He considered his drawings thoughtfully. But the day was almost gone; there wasn't a minute for study now. Taking two sturdy valises from the floor he packed into the first papers that were to be left in England and into the other all he needed for his work in France. The next day he sailed across the Channel.

The first thing he did in Paris was to look up the American poet and diplomat, Mr. Joel Barlow, for whom he carried a letter of introduction. Mr. Barlow read the letter and liked both what it said and the appearance of the young inventor.

"Come with me to dinner," he invited. "Mrs. Barlow will want to meet you and hear news from England." Mrs. Barlow was delighted with their guest. Robert Fulton was then thirty-two years old, tall, handsome, his curly dark hair framing a high, intelligent forehead, his manners agreeable and his conversation interesting. Like Mrs. West, her motherly heart accepted him at once.

"You are to send for your luggage this very night," she said hospitably. "You will like this hotel where we are now I am sure, and soon we shall have our own house. We want you to stay with us! No objections!" She laughed gaily. "Joel, tell him he is to come!"

Robert accepted their invitation, he supposed for a few days. But he lived with the Barlows as a son for seven years until they returned to the United States. During those years they helped him in countless ways and looked after his comfort and health.

One evening some months after his arrival, when his various projects were well under way, Robert brought to Mr. Barlow's library a packet of papers he had placed in his valise the day before leaving England.

"Have you time to look at this, sir?" he asked his friend. And Joel Barlow always made time to hear anything Robert Fulton wanted to talk about.

"It's my newest invention," explained Robert as he showed a sketch of a small, slender oval. This is a design for a cylinder of gunpowder. If this shot is placed *under* a boat it will blow up the vessel. I call it a torpedo from the torpedo fish that kills by a touch. This, you see," he pointed to one end of the oval, "is the timing spring. It sets the powder off at any minute I select. And the torpedo holds enough gunpowder to blow a boat to bits!"

"It sounds barbarous to me, Robert! I'm amazed that you should work on such a thing!" Mr. Barlow's face was shocked and sad. "Though I haven't a doubt you could make it."

"The Duke of Bridgewater thought it cruel, too,"

Robert remembered. "But you see, sir, it will never be necessary to blow up a ship once my invention is proved to be an effective weapon. Even for the test we do not need a good ship. We can use an old, empty hull for that. People will see that a torpedo is sure and deadly and its very *threat* will keep war and piracy from the sea. And once you make the sea safe for rightful travel, sir, you go a long way toward assuring human happiness and progress."

Mr. Barlow studied the sketch. "How will you place this torpedo?"

"I have a design for a boat to travel under water." Robert reached eagerly for more papers. "I call it a submarine boat. It carries the torpedo, places it under the attacked boat and departs before the spring sets off the explosion."

"Like David Bushnell's boat?" asked Mr. Barlow.

"No, mine is quite different. You remember his boat was designed like a turtle's shell with two plates and it rode upstanding in the water. The turtle's head was the small chamber where a man sat in total darkness. I think that was the reason his test failed when he tried to blow up the British *Eagle* in New York harbor during the war for independence. If that man could have seen what he was doing he might have succeeded. Though I do think Bushnell's idea was an improvement over Day's. He had no air and drowned when he made his first test in Plymouth Bay in England the summer of '74. My idea is not original, sir, many men have worked on the problem. But I think my design is vastly improved."

That evening's talk was followed by others with the result that Mr. Barlow was so interested that he advanced money for experiments. But as soon as he built one model, Robert Fulton had a dozen ideas for improvement and started to build another. Materials were costly; Mr. Barlow could not afford to spend more.

In his need, Robert had a new idea. In partnership with a friend he built, in Paris, a great circular building, the first panorama ever built in France. On the huge canvas installed inside he painted a brilliant imaginary scene he called "The Burning of Moscow." It was the kind of painting Benjamin West had taught him to paint and it was immediately successful. People by the hundreds paid admission to see it and it was popular for many years. So vivid was the scene that after the real burning of Moscow, later, some visitors were confused and thought he had painted a real historical scene. Robert was happy for the panorama earned large sums of money, enough to build a model submarine.

This strange boat named the *Nautilus* was ready the summer of 1800. Fulton and one helper holding a candle and a bottle of oxygen descended in the Seine, near Rouen, and stayed under water for twenty minutes.

"We did it sir!" exclaimed the helper proudly when they opened the doorway safely after the ascent. "We did it just as you said!" Fulton smiled happily. Yes, the test was successful.

"We could stay down longer if we could arrange for more air. That messy candle uses too much. We must get rid of it! This afternoon I shall try to cut a window. And a metal container for the oxygen would be better. We could lay it on the bottom, handy."

He installed a four-inch window of glass nearly an inch and a half thick. Descending, he found he could read the hands of his watch so he figured that four such windows would give ample light. Then he made a copper globe for compressed air that was more convenient than the glass jar. Now four men stayed down six hours, a fine demonstration that delighted Robert Fulton and his workers.

Every day that summer he made improvements and tests. The three men who worked with him came to feel no fear under the water and helped him loyally. Robert Fulton's gift for understanding people was one of his greatest helps. Many an inventor has been hindered because he could not get helpers who had imagination and faithfulness. Watt,

Bushnell and others almost failed for this reason. Fulton's men loved him for his kindness and fairness to them. And with all the problems and irritations of new work he never was cross or impatient. They would do anything for him!

Stories of the odd boat at Rouen spread and when the *Nautilus* was towed to Paris for a test there crowds watched from the river banks. Fulton and one assistant descended and stayed under water for twenty minutes, travelling during that time several hundred yards. Thousands cheered wildly when the submarine descended again and reappeared a second time about where it had started.

Fulton now had a hundred new ideas but the season was getting late. Next summer he built a new *Nautilus* that had many original features still in use in modern submarines. Its long cigar shape was enclosed with copper; above the water it looked much like an ordinary boat. There was a mast and sail which folded away for the descent; a heavy metal bar was the keel and strong iron ribs gave support. Oars were set screw-fashion near the middle; anchor and hoisting machinery were forward. Toward the front was a window-lighted conning tower. A long tube supplied the air and copper globes of compressed air were for emergencies.

There were newly designed bombs, too, carrying charges of gunpowder varying from twenty to two

hundred pounds. These needed no timing spring; each had a trigger which set off the bomb the instant it hit the target.

For more than a year, Fulton tried to get government help. He felt that a responsible government should have both the financing and the control of this powerful weapon. His Paris test was made in the hope of interesting Napoleon who did observe it there. Finally an official test was planned.

An old forty-foot sloop was anchored at Brest. Navy men observed while Robert Fulton in his new *Nautilus* advanced and fired a copper bomb containing twenty pounds of gunpowder. The sloop was blown to bits! Tons of water and debris rose skyward and when the sea was calm again nothing remained but the buoy and cable. And the *Nautilus* got safely away.

Fulton and his men were delighted! The skeptical navy men were impressed but, instead of giving him authority to go ahead with the work, the government only promised to pay him if and when he blew up an enemy ship. This was something Fulton had no wish to do. But it seemed necessary for a proof, so all that summer he tried to overtake and blow up a ship but he never succeeded.

This failure discouraged the French government but didn't daunt Robert Fulton. He saw that if he was to make his submarine successful he must develop greater speed and flexibility so that it could travel quickly and secretly.

English friends had kept in touch with his experiments and a couple of years later the Earl of Stanhope invited Fulton to make a test for the British government. They insisted that their own gunners operate the submarine and because of their inexperience the test failed. Later, in 1805 Fulton himself made a test and blew up a large brig near the castle of Prime Minister Pitt. Seventy pounds of gunpowder lifted the brig and scattered her into fragments that sank immediately. Surely *that* was proof! But Pitt died shortly, the government changed and Fulton decided to drop the whole matter for a while. Sometime he would do it; now, perhaps it was better to wait.

Early Steamboats

DISCOURAGEMENT was a word Robert Fulton didn't use. There were a thousand useful things needing to be done in the world. If the time wasn't ripe for one, he could work on another. So, though he was sorry to pack away his plans for a submarine, he was thrilled to have all his days for work on a steam-propelled boat. *There* was something worth doing! Something his own country needed badly!

Probably Robert himself could not have told when the thought of a steamboat first came into his mind. In the part of the country where he was born several men were working on the idea and hundreds discussed it freely. One of the real needs of the new United States was fast, cheap transportation; distances were so great that this was a more serious problem there than in Europe. Flatboats and keelboats were used on rivers and sailing boats on the great lakes. But they were all so slow and uncertain. A trip up the Mississippi from the Gulf to the upper Ohio River took most of a summer and was very expensive.

Two years before Robert was born, a neighbor of the Fultons, William Henry, succeeded in building a steamboat that made two or three short trips. Unfortunately it met with an accident in a storm that wrecked the boat and sank the engine. Mr. Henry was unable to raise any money and so he could not continue his work. His ideas were excellent and Robert had already pondered upon them at the time Deter Gumpf spoke so scornfully that day on the Conestoga.

John Fitch braved the laughter that followed William Henry's disaster and tried to develop a steamboat on the Delaware River during the time that Robert worked in Philadelphia. In the summer of 1786 (just before Robert was twenty-one) he succeeded in getting his steamboat, *The Perseverance*, to make several trips. His great trouble was the same that bothered William Henry; the engine was too large and too heavy for the size of his boat. The machinery not only took too much space but it was so heavy that the boat rode low in the water and made it impossible to carry enough freight and passengers to pay expenses. The boat was very costly to run and though Fitch had ideas for many improvements, he had spent all his own money on this boat and as he was unable to get more capital he had to give up his project.

That same summer James Rumsey propelled a boat by steam at the rate of four miles an hour. This was on the Potomac and George Washington was among those who watched and applauded the test.

Later John Stevens, of New Jersey, who was an admirer of John Fitch, made a long series of experiments and then built two steamboats that had many original ideas still in use. As early as 1774 Samuel Morey had made a run with his boat from Hartford to New York City. There were dozens of other men in Europe as well as in the United States who were working and making progress on this problem.

At that time the United States had no patent system. Each state gave patents. This encouraged many inventors but it did not give opportunity to see what others had already done. Many a man worked years at a problem some other inventor had solved.

Probably Robert Fulton, in England, knew relatively little about all this work done in his own country. There was no press service or radio to carry news. But he often discussed steam navigation with his English friends. The Earl of Stanhope had an idea of his own. He would use the form of a duck's foot and make a paddle that would close on the forward movement and open for the backward push that would send the boat through the water. The friends often argued for hours about this, the Duke of Bridgewater wondering if such a craft could be used on his canals.

Fulton thought to propel a boat by using the principle of the spring in a salmon's tail. But when he tried this on a model in 1793 he found that the boat moved by jerks, a rapid forward motion which came almost to a stop, then another forward motion. So, remembering the paddles on Deter Gumpf's scow, he decided to use side paddles. His idea was ingenious and original; he figured that by revolving the paddles he would keep them out of the water all the time they were not actually propelling the boat and so save the drag of other inventors propellers. He made many toy boats to test paddles of different shapes and sizes; to see whether three or four or six worked better and to study problems of resistance and motion. It was in connection with these studies that he wrote to Boulton and Watt about the costs of an engine in November of 1794.

In Paris his good friend Joel Barlow introduced him to an American named Robert R. Livingston who was then United States minister to France. It was he who, as Chancellor of the New York Court of Chancery, administered the oath of office to George Washington when he became the first President of the United States. Mr. Livingston was so interested in the steamboat idea that he became Robert Fulton's equal partner.

Because of his wide acquaintance and knowledge of men and affairs, Mr. Livingston was able to raise money for experiments. This help, coming after his difficulties with the submarine, made Robert very happy. He set to work at once to build a steamboat.

This boat was about seventy feet long and eight feet wide and it was thought to be very strong. The partners rented an engine as it would take months to have one built for them in England. The boat lay at dock on the Seine while Robert Fulton and his mechanics worked long hours installing the precious engine. At last everything seemed ready and the partners set a day for the test.

One evening just before the date set for the test, Mr. Fulton came home weary but happy. Hardly was he inside the door before a workman, breathless with running, followed him.

"The engine's gone to the bottom, sir!" he cried in shocked tones.

Mr. Fulton hurried back to the dock with him— and sure enough! The boat was broken and the costly engine had slid to the bottom of the river.

Robert Fulton pulled off his coat and, forgetting weariness, worked right through the night with his men. Not once did he stop for rest until the engine was rescued and set safely on deck. He never did discover exactly what had caused the accident. Perhaps a wind storm shortly before had weakened the boat; it was now too wrecked to make sure even of that.

New plans were made and the boat was rebuilt. But all this cost heavily in time and money and energy. It cost popular support, too, for docks were crowded

daily with people who watched and criticized and
jeered. They would not forget the sight of a boat split
in two and of the dripping engine.

Finally the ninth of August was set for a test
and docks were packed with curious crowds.

"She looks like a chariot with a stove in the middle," some one shouted as the fireman built a fire
under the boiler and smoke poured from the stack.

But laughter turned to silent awe when the "chariot," without sail or oars, moved away from the
dock at about the speed of a man walking. Even
the great Napoleon took notice of this test and is
said to have remarked, "This is capable of chang-
ing the face of the world!"

Fulton was disappointed that he could not make
more speed but otherwise he was very happy about

this test. Now they had accomplished the first big step of their undertaking. The new type of boiler used, an original idea of his, brought water to steam quicker than any used before and was proved satisfactory. He felt sure, now, that steam could move a larger boat and that with added comfort as well as speed, a steamboat could be run as a successful business investment.

At once Mr. Livingston began correspondence with authorities in New York State and secured the right for himself and his partner to build and operate steamboats on the Hudson for twenty years. There was a bit of a joker though, for in voting permission, the legislature said that boats must be able to move at least four miles per hour against the current—a requirement *they* thought quite impossible of fulfilling.

But to Robert Fulton, practically nothing seemed impossible. As soon as the permit arrived, he ordered from Boulton and Watt an engine to be built by his own design and to be delivered to the United States. Three years passed before it reached the port of New York for there were legal difficulties as well as delayed shipping because of war conditions in Europe. But all that time, Robert was studying, planning, working, determined that he would build a steamboat which should be a business success in his own country and sure that he could do it.

The Clermont

SAILING home to America in the autumn of 1806 Robert Fulton must have thought over the many changes twenty years had made. His mother had died seven years before so she would not be there to greet him. But she had lived long enough to know that the modest young painter had developed into an inventor of distinction. She had had the great happiness of knowing that her son was doing useful work and earning honor, friends and fortune.

Some of his close friends were now in the United States. He hoped to land in time to celebrate his birthday with the Joel Barlows in their beautiful home in Washington but the ship was delayed—sailing took as long as it did twenty years before—and so that pleasure was impossible. He stayed in New York and set to work at once on the steamboat. Later he planned to offer his designs for torpedoes and submarines to his own government at Washington and to try to interest them in canals to help overland transportation.

He made arrangements for building the hull in a shipyard on East River and made a careful inspection of his engine. It had finally arrived and was

stored in Mr. Barker's warehouse on South Street.
Work went along well and in the spring the hull
was launched and the engine carted over and installed.

Robert Fulton worked daily with his men and, as
usual, won their interest and devotion. But as the
boat neared completion, observers on the docks were
not so kindly. There were many petty acts of de-
struction, some plain thievery, others perhaps inspired by jealousy of his progress and possibly by
sailors who feared to lose their livelihood if the
steamboat should happen to be a success. His men
took turns watching but finally Fulton had to hire
a watchman to insure safety during the night. This
troubled him as he had always managed to get along
well with onlookers.

His partner, Robert Livingston, was in New York
now and came frequently to watch progress. As a
gesture of gratitude to him, Robert Fulton had decided to name his steamboat the *Clermont*, the name
of Mr. Livingston's beautiful country home on the
Hudson River.

People who lingered around the docks called the
boat "Fulton's Folly" and promised themselves fun
when they could say, "I told you it would never
work!" Robert often heard them making sarcastic
remarks, but he paid no attention. This wasn't the
first of such chatter he had heard—though he might

have hoped for more understanding in his own country.

The *Clermont* was one hundred and fifty feet long, about thirteen feet wide and drew two feet of water. The two paddle wheels were set a bit in front of the center, one at each side. They splashed in and out of the water making a great spray when in motion. The engine was in plain sight; a railing with seats ran almost around the deck and a low, covered cabin was at the back. Robert Fulton seems to have been the first designer who realized that travel might be more than merely getting some place —it might be fun. So in the *Clermont* he made sure there were comfortable seats where passengers could enjoy the view.

As the time neared for the test, he and Mr. Livingston invited friends to make the journey to Albany with them. Food for all was taken on board for it was to be a real celebration. Many of Mr. Livingston's relatives were invited, among them two sisters, Helen and Kate, who were his cousins. Helen Livingston wrote a letter to her mother about the invitation and added, "Mr. Fulton says it will be something to remember all our lives."

Late in the afternoon of August ninth, Fulton, unknown to any but his trusted mechanics, went to the dock where the *Clermont* lay, got up steam and rode, successfully, around to East River. But he wasn't satisfied with the speed. He anchored and put on another pair of paddles, tried those and was better pleased.

"Look at her!" he shouted to his men as they steamed off again. "Did you ever see a boat answer to her helm as this one does? I've turned her now three times in her own length!" Then he listened to the engine carefully and went over the whole boat looking for a chance to make improvements.

"Notice that sloop, sir?" one of his men remarked as the *Clermont* steamed back to her dock. "We're passing her that easy! She'll soon be lying there, for the breeze is dying fast. But we're going right along."

This day was the anniversary of the trial on the Seine four years before. Now Robert Fulton had a boat more than twice as big, a better engine and every prospect of success.

At one o'clock Monday afternoon on August the seventeenth, 1807, the *Clermont*, under a full head of steam, was ready for the trip to Albany. It was a fine summer day and crowds had come to watch Fulton prove his "Folly." On board the guests were looking serious instead of gay. Of course it would all be very well if the thing worked. But getting good clothes wet would be a nuisance if the boat split in two as others had. And *how* people would poke fun at them!

The bell rang. Ropes were cast off. Mr. Fulton gave the signal to start. The engine turned—people held their breath—it stopped! There wasn't a sound but the gentle lapping of the river against the boat.

Crowds began to jeer—the dock was jammed with people.

"Told you she wouldn't go!"

"Look at Fulton's Folly! Speedy! Watch 'er go!"

Even the passengers murmured and wondered, though they made a pretense of politeness. Ladies gathered up their skirts and drifted toward the stern, away from the engine. Gentlemen stood by the railing around the engine and looked down at the thing with vexation.

"I wish we were well out of this," some one whispered.

"Bob has had many a bee in his bonnet before this but his steam folly will prove the worst yet!" said another, shaking his head.

Robert Fulton stepped onto one of the seats built for passengers and spoke loudly enough to be heard on the dock.

"Do not be distressed, friends. I cannot now tell you what the matter is but if you will give me half an hour, I shall get us going or we shall abandon the trip for the day." Then he went down to the engine and began a careful check for trouble. In strained silence people watched and waited. He

found what was amiss, corrected it, and in a very few minutes the paddles began to turn. The *Clermont* moved.

People on the dock stared in silent wonder. Robert Fulton stood motionless, his hand on the rail by the engine, his head bent listening to the "chug, chug, chug," of his engine. Slowly the boat steamed away from the dock at a speed between four and five miles an hour. The flag of the United States of America with its thirteen stripes and circle of fifteen stars fluttered gaily in the head-on breeze from the north. The journey to Albany began.

Suddenly the frightened silence of the onlookers ended in a cheer of joy that echoed from boat to shore and back again. People tossed hats in air; shouted; hugged each other gleefully. Passengers' faces relaxed into smiles. They now recalled that they were the guests of a famous inventor. They rushed to shake his hand and to congratulate him. They were hysterical with relief, excitement and joy.

The American Citizen, a New York newspaper, had carried an announcement of the trial trip and that, and of course word that had passed from person to person, drew great crowds to the river banks all along the city. Many of the curious expected to say, "Well of course! I knew he never could do it!" as they went away. Instead, they stayed to watch with wonder and joy as the amazing boat splashed steadily up stream. It had masts, but no sails; it sprayed showers of water like fountains at either side and every time a fireman tossed more pine logs into the firebox, sparks and pitch-black smoke poured from the tall stack.

Fishermen in small boats stared in terror. Then hastily gathering in their nets they rowed desperately for shore. This was the worst sea monster they'd ever heard of—angry, too, and spitting fire and flame! They couldn't get away fast enough and the stories they told their families lived in the countryside for generations.

Little Sarah Barker was on board the *Clermont* with her father; it was in his warehouse that the engine had been stored while the hull was being built and she had been especially invited by Mr. Fulton. Her little feet swung from the seat that had been fixed for her comfort and she smoothed her petticoats proudly. She was glad the boat was going and people were gay. It looked as though they all thought Mr. Fulton was the great man her father said he was. Anyway it was fun to ride on the river and hear people shout.

Mr. Fulton looked at her and smiled. Sarah was a little younger than Peggy had been that day she stood on the bank of the Conestoga, hands full of spring flowers, and watched Deter Gumpf's scow move as the paddles turned. He smiled as Sarah clapped her hands gleefully, and wished that Mary and Isabelle and Peggy could have been aboard. But Lancaster was a long journey from New York in 1807. He turned back to watch his engine. It was performing splendidly and progress up the river was steady.

Afterward Robert Fulton often spoke of that August Monday as the happiest day of his life. He was almost forty-two years old, tall, handsome, kindly, loved by many friends. His heart warmed as he thought of a secret happiness that was even more important to him than the success of the *Clermont*. News of that would come soon!

All afternoon and evening the boat steamed and splashed on. Supper was a party which Mr. Livingston and Mr. Fulton had provided and was a real feast. The ham and roasted chickens, buttered rusks and gingerbread, green apple tarts, pound cake, spice cookies and fresh early plums from Mr. Livingston's orchard tasted marvelously well, when eaten on the deck. As twilight fell, the guests joined in singing, and a favorite was the Scotch ballad Robert Fulton loved, "Ye Banks and Braes o' Bonny Doon"

"Ye banks and braes 'o Bonny Doon,
How can ye bloom so fresh and fair;
How can ye chant, ye little birds,
And I sae weary fu' of care?"

Occasional stops were made, as the *Clermont* did not have room enough to carry firewood for the entire journey. As the boat approached the wharf, one of the crew blew a long horn (there was no whistle) and as soon as the boat touched the dock, men dashed ashore and hastily loaded the fuel.

For the night the ladies made themselves as comfortable as was possible in the cabin at the stern while the gentlemen stayed on the deck. The dim, candle-lighted cabin must have seemed a strange place. The unaccustomed sounds of steam and water would not help toward restful sleep! Breakfast was served the next morning and still the boat chugged on.

At one o'clock on Tuesday they arrived opposite Clermont, Mr. Livingston's estate one hundred and ten miles from New York City. As the boat turned toward the dock, Mr. Livingston stood at the bow and announced the engagement of his beautiful niece, Harriet Livingston, and his partner, Robert Fulton. Harriet was on board and as she stood beside Robert to receive congratulations and good wishes, friends thought they never had seen such a handsome couple. She would be a good wife for the inventor for in addition to beauty and family connections she was a skilful harpist, an artist and she had many friends.

The gay, happy party went ashore and Mr. Livingston entertained them royally. They stayed for dinner and supper and a good night's sleep. The crew, on board, had a rest too, though Captain Brink took time off in the evening to row across the river and bring back his wife. He had promised her that she should ride to Albany in a "boat driven by a tea kettle!"

At nine the next morning the *Clermont* with all aboard left for Albany where they arrived at five that same evening—a total journey of one hundred and fifty miles in thirty-two hours running time. Returning to New York, the trip started at nine on Thursday morning and the hour between six and seven was spent at Mr. Livingston's. Arrival in New York was at four Friday afternoon—thirty hours of running time.

The whole journey had been a brilliant success. But in writing his report to Mr. Barlow in Washington, Robert Fulton modestly said, "My steamboat voyage to Albany and back has turned out rather more favorably than I had calculated."

Later Work

AFTER the successful journey to Albany, Robert Fulton kept the *Clermont* at the dock in New York for two weeks while he checked over every part and made improvements that had occurred to him. Then he and his partner announced regular trips, and handbills were given out telling hours, prices and other particulars.

They planned three round trips each fortnight and the fare charged was the same as on sailboats. The trip up was to start at eight in the morning. "Dinner will be served up exactly at 2 o'clock; tea, with meats, which is also supper, at 8 in the evening; breakfast at 9 in the morning; no one has any claim on the steward for victuals at any other hour."

Evidently it was expected that some passengers would ride short distances, for the handbill says, "Way passengers who are not out for more than half the night are not entitled to lie down in a berth." These way passengers were advised to be at the docks along the route an hour before the scheduled time because wind and tide might vary the time of the boat's arrival.

Berths were to be kept tidy, as this notice shows: "It is not permitted for any person to lie down in a berth with their boots or shoes on, under penalty of one dollar and a half, and half a dollar fine for every half hour they offend against this rule.

"A shelf has been added to each berth on which gentlemen will please put their boots, shoes and clothes that the cabin may not be encumbered."

All this thought for food, cleanliness and the comfort of the passengers was an amazing novelty— and very elegant, too. Robert Fulton realized that travel would be more popular if people were comfortable while on the way. All the luxury of travel by train and boat today is an outgrowth of his idea. People *enjoyed* his boats. That helped to make his venture successful.

Many stories are handed down about the early trips of the *Clermont*. Some come from letters written about that time and later discovered in attics. Others are told and retold and likely lose nothing in the repetitions.

One story tells of a party of Indians on the west bank of the Hudson. They saw what they thought was an angry monster roaring up the river and dropped to their knees to beg the Great Spirit for safety. But as the monster splashed on, they depended on their own heels and ran west till many miles lay between them and the river.

The owner of a small sawmill came to the dock when the *Clermont* stopped for firewood.

"Looks like you've got a sawmill here!" he said to Captain Brink.

"So it does," replied the captain.

"Perhaps I could put *my* sawmill on a scow and take her to the forest. Sounds easier than bringing the logs to the mill."

One old letter says that when the *Clermont* reached the garrison at West Point all the soldiers came to the bank and cheered as the boat passed by.

Fishermen shouted and stormed against the steamboat. They thought the noise would frighten fish from the river. Farmers complained that the smoke would discolor their sheeps' wool. River sloops were careless and sometimes really vicious, about running into the boat and many times the paddles were damaged. Other sailors, less courageous, ran their boats ashore and took to the woods.

But the *Clermont* continued to make her regular trips. On the first voyage down from Albany, Fulton had announced that any who wished could take passage. Only two men, and these, as it happened, Frenchmen, were brave enough to accept. Now each trip carried forty-five to sixty paying passengers. In October the *New York Evening Post* daringly suggested that now regular service was established perhaps the *Clermont* should carry the United States

mail and thus speed delivery. When autumn storms
began, the *Clermont* was taken off and during the
winter was rebuilt.

In the spring, renamed the *North River*, she
again began regular trips and was in service for several years. During the summer of 1808 a sister
ship, *The Car of Neptune*, was built and now there
was service from both New York and Albany twice
each week. Soon after a third boat, *The Paragon*,
was built and put in service. This was the best of
the three, for Robert Fulton added new features.

With the development of New York City and
Jersey ports, a better mode of travel was needed in
the harbor. Sailboats and hand-paddle craft were
slow and uncertain. Robert Fulton invented a ferry
boat which he called a "twin boat" because two hulls
were joined by a deck platform for carriages and
horses. The boat had rounded ends like the ferries
of today, so that time need not be wasted turning
around. He also invented a kind of fender to lessen
the shock of hitting the dock. He built two of these
ferries and christened them *The York* and *The Jersey*
and they were very popular.

He made some progress with his ideas for canal
navigation, too. In the spring of 1807, President
Thomas Jefferson invited him to go to Mississippi
and see if he thought a canal could be built connect-
ing Lake Pontchartrain with the Mississippi River.

That was a victory! How he wanted to go! But he was needed daily in the New York shipyard where the *Clermont* was building and also for constant supervision of work on a torpedo test set for July. Much as he wished to accept, he could not undertake new work that spring, so he regretfully declined the President's invitation.

Friends often said of Robert Fulton "he was never so happy as when he had two or three ideas working in his mind." During all the time that he was building the *Clermont* and trying to interest the President and Congress in canal navigation, he did not forget his submarines. Mr. Barlow talked with Secretary of State James Madison, and Secretary of the Navy Robert Smith, and Mr. Fulton did a small experiment for them in Rock Creek near Washington. This interested them so much that he put on a series of experiments for them, the most important one taking place in New York harbor July 20, 1807—just four weeks before the *Clermont* first went to Albany. The Fulton torpedo, fired from a submarine boat, blew up a brig and scattered the fragments.

Robert Fulton thought this was proof enough but Congress was a long time in allowing money for more work. Even though he never had the satisfaction of building a submarine for his own country, he knew his work made the government think more about protecting the high seas. And he did design and build the first steam-propelled warship for the United States.

Through all the busy years of painting and inventing, his personal life was happy as his boyhood had been. His years in Europe brought him many rare friendships. His marriage to Harriet Livingston a few months after the first trip of the *Clermont* was very happy and he was proud of their four children, Robert Barlow, Julia, Mary and Cornelia Livingston. Mrs. Fulton was a gracious hostess and Mr. Fulton loved their evenings together or with friends in their comfortable home in New York City.

Many an evening as the little family sat before the sitting-room fire, Mrs. Livingston played and her husband had an hour of rest. Then the children would beg for stories of his boyhood in Lancaster and their father told them of his mother and sisters and brother.

"Tell us about the first day you went to school," Julia begged, one evening.

"I'd rather hear about how Mary made the candles," Mary Fulton's namesake asked, practically. "Were they like our candles, Father?"

Mr. Fulton looked at the tall, graceful candles burning in crystal holders on the mantel and smiled.

"Not as perfectly made, Mary," he admitted, "but they gave good light."

"I'd like to hear about the boat with paddles.

You called it the *George Washington*, didn't you, Father?" young Robert Barlow asked. "Was it hard to turn the paddles?"

"Yes, it was hard—but easier than poling, at that!" his father answered. "And boys always wanted to do that job! Sit here, Julia, while I tell you about it." And they heard again their favorite story. As it ended, Mrs. Livingston tilted her harp and softly played the notes of their evening song.

"I wish I'd lived then!" Small Robert's eyes sparkled as he stood on the hearthrug and stared at his father adoringly. "You had a war and prisoners and fishing and everything that's fun! Now we just live in a city!"

"Don't say that, son!" Robert Fulton exclaimed. "You live at a better time! You will have more education and culture; your country will be safe from war because enemies will not dare come near its shores! All people will be happier because the seas will be safe and free!" His eyes sparkled as he smiled at them. "And someday, maybe you'll see a steamboat cross the ocean!"

"*Really*, Father? You think of wonderful things!"

IN A USEFUL LIFE

the boy from the Conestoga valley did much besides paint pictures and design a steamboat.

For *bettering canal transportation he invented:*

A machine for cutting marble (marble was used for piers and locks)
A machine for spinning flax (ropes for pulling boat were made of flax)
A machine for making rope
A system of inclined planes to replace locks
A dredging cart
A system of cast-iron bridges and aqueducts
New types of canal boats
A market boat (sometimes called a passage boat)
A despatch boat for express service
A trader boat
A new method for taking a canal boat across a river
A perpendicular lift (for passing boats in a canal)
A descending table (another method of passing)

For *making water travel comfortable, safe and fast he designed:*

The *Clermont*, the first commercially successful steamboat.

Other steamboats he designed and built were:

The Car of Neptune	*The Paragon*
The Firefly	*The Richmond*
The Washington	*The York* (a ferry boat)
The Vesuvius	*The Nassau* (a ferry boat)

The Fulton   *The Olive Branch*
Fulton the First (the first   *The Chancellor Livingston*
    steam warship)   *The Mute*
The Emperor of Russia (the only boat of his design not
    intended for use in his own country)

For *enforcing the "Liberty of the Seas,"* he tried to make
weapons so powerful that war and piracy would be impossible. He invented:

Torpedoes
Submarine guns
An air gun
A cable cutter (to cut cables of enemy boats at anchor)
The first submarine plunging boat

"Where there is a need, find out how to supply it."—
Robert Fulton.

Clermont 1807

Nautilus 1800

Fulton 1813

Car of Neptune 1807

Fire Fly 1812

Richmond 1813

967 F.W.